OECD Health Policy Studies

Health for the People, by the People

BUILDING PEOPLE-CENTRED HEALTH SYSTEMS

OECD

BETTER POLICIES FOR BETTER LIVES

This work is published under the responsibility of the Secretary-General of the OECD. The opinions expressed and arguments employed herein do not necessarily reflect the official views of the Members of the OECD.

This document, as well as any data and map included herein, are without prejudice to the status of or sovereignty over any territory, to the delimitation of international frontiers and boundaries and to the name of any territory, city or area.

The statistical data for Israel are supplied by and under the responsibility of the relevant Israeli authorities. The use of such data by the OECD is without prejudice to the status of the Golan Heights, East Jerusalem and Israeli settlements in the West Bank under the terms of international law.

Please cite this publication as:
OECD (2021), *Health for the People, by the People: Building People-centred Health Systems* , OECD Health Policy Studies, OECD Publishing, Paris, *https://doi.org/10.1787/c259e79a-en*.

ISBN 978-92-64-37912-1 (print)
ISBN 978-92-64-47545-8 (pdf)

OECD Health Policy Studies
ISSN 2074-3181 (print)
ISSN 2074-319X (online)

Foreword

At the 2017 OECD Ministerial Conference on the Next Generation of Health Reforms, Ministers called for improved efforts to strengthen the people-centredness of health systems. No recent event has more clearly demonstrated this need than the global COVID-19 pandemic. COVID-19 highlighted pre-existing weaknesses and failures of health systems, and underscored the need for improved analytical tools to help policy makers define how health systems are held accountable for performance and patient-centredness.

This includes ongoing work to develop a new generation of indicators that measure the outcomes and experiences of health care that matter most to people through the Patient-Reported Indicators Surveys (PaRIS), including the PaRIS International Survey for People Living with Chronic Conditions, as well as policy-oriented research aimed to develop a cross-country understanding of the extent to which person-centred policy making has taken hold in health systems.

This report is intended to respond to the urgent need for improved conceptual tools and analysis of how health systems deliver for the people who use them. It presents an OECD Framework and Scorecard for People-Centred Health Systems to help policy makers better understand health policy problems, from the perspective of the people. Five dimensions of people-centredness for health systems – voice, choice, co-production, integration and respectfulness – are identified as critical building blocks for a people-centred system. The report benchmarks the progress countries have made towards a more people-centred approach to health. It finds that despite widespread agreement on the importance of people-centredness, no countries have comprehensively implemented people-centred policies across all essential dimensions.

The report further applies the lens of people-centredness to examine the enormous impact that COVID-19 has had on people and health systems in OECD countries and beyond. It draws special attention to the impact of the COVID-19 pandemic on people-centredness, and discusses key policies to help move the needle towards more people-centred health systems in the OECD area, which are critical in both "normal" times and during health shocks and crises. It finds that countries have largely overlooked people-centredness in their pandemic response, underscoring the distance still to go to fully embed people-centred policy making in health systems.

This publication was prepared by the OECD Health Division under the co-ordination of Frederico Guanais and Elina Suzuki. It would not have been possible without the support of Nick Tomlinson, Michael van den Berg, Katherine de Bienassis, Gabriel di Paolantonio, José Bijlholt, and Tom Raitzik Zonenschein, and was aided immensely by input from Francesca Colombo, Mark Pearson, and Stefano Scarpetta. The authors would like to further extend their gratitude to the participants in the Health Committee and the many policy makers across OECD and partner countries who gave their time to responding to policy questionnaires and reviewing and commenting on draft chapters. This report would not have been possible without their generosity.

Table of contents

FIGURES

TABLES

Follow OECD Publications on:

http://twitter.com/OECD_Pubs

http://www.facebook.com/OECDPublications

http://www.linkedin.com/groups/OECD-Publications-4645871

http://www.youtube.com/oecdilibrary

OECD Alerts http://www.oecd.org/oecddirect/

Executive summary

The push to make health systems more accountable to the people who use them – in other words, to make health systems more *people-centred* – is not a new effort. Health professionals, policy makers and patients themselves have long realised that the institutions making up health systems today are no longer fit for purpose, neither meeting the needs of those who use them, nor sufficiently adaptable to rapidly developing global trends, including digitalisation, population ageing and pandemic shocks.

This report examines the steps OECD countries have taken to put people-centredness into action across health systems, including their institutions, workforce, governance and decision-making. The OECD Framework for People-Centred Health Systems includes five dimensions – voice, choice, co-production, integration and respectfulness – that can be used to methodically analyse people-centredness. An application of relevant indicators to this framework to benchmark how countries have embedded people-centredness in their health systems reveals that despite broad support for a people-centred health systems agenda, few countries have comprehensively institutionalised people-centred policies across these five key dimensions. Moreover, despite recent progress in developing patient-reported measures, regularly collected indicators for people-centredness are still vastly insufficient.

Policies to address COVID-19 paid little heed to the needs of people-centred health services, especially in the early phases of the pandemic

The health systems response to the COVID-19 pandemic over the last two years was largely *not* people-centred, reflecting the reality that policy changes towards people-centred care have not been deeply embedded into institutions. Yet the speed at which policies were introduced or adapted to deal with the pandemic suggests that with sufficient will, there is opportunity for progress to strengthen a people-centred agenda.

- People-centredness was very weak in public communications about the state of scientific evidence and recommendations for preventive behaviours, such as the use of facemasks and the uptake in vaccination, with misinformation impacting vaccine hesitancy. By late April 2021, the proportion of unvaccinated people who were unwilling to receive a vaccine reached 29% in Germany, 34% in Australia, and 54% in the United States.
- Integration and continuity of care suffered greatly during various waves of the pandemic, with diagnostic services and treatment of patients with non-COVID-19 needs disrupted or delayed. More often than not, there were no instruments to prioritise continuity of care for patients at risk or those living with chronic diseases. Delays in cancer screening and diagnosis have been common, including an average 5 percentage point decline in breast cancer screening over the previous two years in 2020 compared with 2019 across seven OECD countries with available data, and delays in cancer diagnosis reported in at least 12 OECD countries.
- Respectfulness for patients and their families also suffered. For example, all countries adopted strong restrictions on visits to people hospitals and long-term care facilities, in many cases even at

the end of life, upending traditional norms around respectful end-of-life care. These restrictions were implemented to protect long-term care residents and workers from COVID-19 infections but also affected the experience of many who died of COVID-19, given that more than 40% of all COVID-19-related deaths across 25 OECD countries took place among long-term care residents. Although most countries later changed these policies following popular outcry, the experience of deaths among long-term care facilities residents away from their family was dramatic.

- Despite these shortcomings, there were important signs and opportunities for future progress, such as the acceleration of real-time data sharing, linkage of health data to follow patient pathways across health systems, and the adoption of digital technologies to overcome disruptions.

- People's preferences also evolved over the pandemic and digital tools have helped communication and the roll-out of policies to incentivise vaccination rates. Since the start of the pandemic, 34 of 38 OECD countries or subnational regions have adopted variations of COVID-19 passes requiring proof of vaccination status, a negative COVID-19 test, or recovery from previous infection to access public spaces or engage in certain activities.

- The absence of formal patient representation in health decision making was particularly conspicuous when countries needed to make rapid decisions to contain the virus's spread, such as measures restricting mobility and measures implemented in hospitals and long-term care settings. Among 57 patient organisations in Europe, nearly two-thirds of respondents (63%) indicated that there was no patient involvement or consultation in management and decision-making processes during the pandemic.

Despite some progress, no country yet delivers strong, person-centred care across all key policy domains of the OECD Scorecard

The patterns observed during the response to the COVID-19 pandemic are not surprising when the dimensions of people-centredness across countries are examined from a broader health systems perspective. The measured results within the five dimensions of the OECD Framework and Scorecard on People-Centred Health Systems highlight weaknesses that preceded the pandemic and underscore the mixed progress in the journey towards people-centred health systems.

- **With few exceptions, patient voice remains weakly embedded in decision-making processes.** Just 11% (3/27) of countries reported that patients had a formal role in at least four of five key decision-making areas of health policy. While patient voice is broadly recognised as important for personal health decision-making, fewer countries included patients in decision-making around health care research or funding for research.

- **Countries have improved patients choice across many health services, but access and affordability continue to act as barriers for many people.** While provider choice is widespread, access and affordability constraints affect free choice. Across 23 OECD countries, one in six adults reported delaying or foregoing care due to cost.

- **Patients are increasingly seeking control over their health information, to better influence their own health and the health care they receive.** Digital tools offer the potential to greatly expand patient access to their own information. Yet while the majority of OECD countries (70%) say they are implementing ways for people to access their health data electronically, in 2020 just two-fifths (43%) allowed patients to interact with their personal health information. Moreover, health and digital literacy remain low for many people, with poor health literacy reported by more than half of the population in two-thirds of OECD countries.

- **Countries have leveraged digital tools to improve integration.** Despite progress in the uptake of electronic health records, establishing linkages and integration between electronic records has been slow, with primary care often excluded from close electronic integration with other parts of the health system. Fewer than 40% of countries reported they regularly conducted linkage projects with primary care data.

- **Measurement of patient experience and outcomes is far from systematic in most countries, and international comparability remains limited.** Much recent focus on strengthening people-centred measures of health systems has been on expanding patient-reported measures. Other dimensions, such as including patients in decision-making processes and ensuring patient access and choice, are also important components of people-centred care, and must be measured accordingly. The lack of regularly-collected data to measure progress underscores how far many countries have to go to better embed people-centredness into their health systems.

1 An analytical framework and scorecard for people-centred health systems

This chapter presents the OECD Framework for People-Centred Health Systems and discusses the results of a benchmarking exercise and patient-level analysis that uses existing health data related to people-centred care – across the domains of voice, choice, co-production, integration, and respectfulness. Results of the Scorecard underscore the importance of all five dimensions presented in the Framework, and find that while people-centredness is relatively well embedded in certain dimensions – notably choice and respectfulness – no country delivers strongly people-centred care across all policy areas. Moreover, the lack of strong cross-country data in certain dimensions highlights the need to improve the collection of data to measure people-centredness: not only through scaling up the systematic collection and reporting of patient-reported measures, but also through better capturing the extent of people-centredness at the governance and systems level.

Economic growth and social progress have driven major gains in health in recent decades, with life expectancy at birth rising by more than 13 years on average across OECD countries since the Organisation was created in 1960. This progress is unquestionably one of the greatest success stories of the 20th century. At the same time, it has meant that the challenges faced by health systems today are in many cases different from the challenges these systems were developed to address.

The rising burden of non-communicable diseases offers a key example of this challenge. Successful fight against infectious diseases has led to non-communicable diseases – including cardiovascular disease, cancer, and diabetes – becoming the leading causes of death and disease globally. Yet despite this epidemiological shift, health systems have not necessarily shifted their focus. Only about 3% of total health expenditure is spent on prevention, including prevention of risk factors for chronic non-communicable diseases and core public health functions to respond to threats from emerging infection diseases.

Similarly, improvements in health have contributed to gains in life expectancy and the population ageing is now driving major demographic shifts. Since 2000, life expectancy at birth in OECD countries has increased by more than four years, from 76.9 to 81 years. At the same time, the proportion of the population aged 65 years and older in OECD countries is rising fast and now represents more than 17% of the population on average. This demographic change has brought with it a rise in health conditions and diseases associated with ageing, including Alzheimer's and other dementias. It has also increased the need for long-term care services, both at home and in care facilities. These factors, together with rising costs associated with new health care technology, are driving further health spending growth, raising total health spending, now accounting for 8.8% of GDP, on average across OECD countries (prior to the COVID-19 pandemic), and projected to rise to 10.2% of GDP by 2030.

The COVID-19 pandemic has compounded such structural pressures, as health systems must be able not only to maintain continuity of regular services for chronic patients, but also to quickly detect and contain emergent infectious diseases. Continuity of services requires surge capacity and an ability to secure supplies of essential goods in times of disruption. Strong essential public health functions such as surveillance, testing and contact tracing, laboratory capacity, data collection and data sharing, preparations for large scale vaccination need to be managed at speed and scale. Similarly, the pandemic has highlighted the need for strong people's capabilities to manage their own health and population buy-in and responsiveness to implement containment measures.

Against this already complex scenario, the expectation of what health care systems should provide has also risen. These rising expectations has been driven not only by higher incomes but also increasing access to information, including information available through digital technology. People today are better able than ever to seek information about their health and the care they receive, and to challenge health systems to deliver better care. More educated and internet-savvy health system users today may be far less tolerant of the *doctor knows best* approach which dominated health care in the 20th century.

Demographic change, the advancement of digital technologies, the epidemiological shift towards NCDs and the threat of emergent infectious diseases, together with rising expectations over what health systems should deliver require **health systems to become more responsive to the people who use them.** The growing expectation that people will have a say in decisions about their care requires a systemic shift towards a more person-centred approach. Similarly, non-communicable diseases and age-related health conditions often require a long-term, co-ordinated approach to help manage and care for chronic diseases. By equipping people with the right information and motivation, a people-centred health system can help health service users make wiser health choices. Moving towards people-centred systems also represents a move towards a shared responsibility, encouraging people, where they are able to do so, to take responsibility for maintaining their own health and for contributing to collective efforts to tackle public health threats.

While countries have made significant progress towards putting in place policies that advance a people-centred health systems agenda, progress remains uneven, and thinking around people-centredness too often takes a siloed approach, overlooking how different dimensions of the health system must work together to deliver truly people-centred care.

The OECD Framework for People-Centred Health Systems

People-centred care is not a new concept. Putting people at the centre has been a priority for health systems in recent decades. The importance of including patients in their own care was recognised in the 1978 Alma Ata Declaration among other global health commitments. There has been extensive discussion – in the literature and by practitioners and patients – of what matters for people-centred care and what building blocks are needed to achieve it. At the same time, there is no universally agreed-upon definition of what constitutes a people-centred health system, let alone what is needed to accomplish it.

In part, this is due to the necessary complexity of providing care that is responsive to the individual person. What matters for some people may be seen to be unnecessary or objectionable for others; moreover, an individual's needs are not static, and preferences may change over time (Health Foundation., 2016[1]). The notion of who is at the centre of the health system has itself also changed: the original concept of 'patient-centred' care has arguably evolved beyond a focus on just patients, to more holistically consider the broader context of the individual, their families, and other carers (Santana et al., 2018[2]). The interpretation of 'people-centredness' has also differed in different contexts: In the United Kingdom and Canada, for example, the idea of 'patient-centred medicine' has been associated with primary care, while in the United States, patient-centred care emerged primarily from the patient's rights movement (Nolte, Merkur and Anell, 2020[3]). The World Health Organization by its turn emphasises the central role of integration in the concept of people-centredness (World Health Organization Regional Office for Europe, 2016[4]).

There have been multiple, often overlapping efforts in the literature to identify and categorise the key components of people-centredness. While differences have emerged in the terminology used around the concepts of 'people-centred care', many of these different definitions share common themes. There is much consistency in terms of what the people-centred health system entails: placing people, their families, and communities at the heart of health systems, empowering them, building care around the needs and expectations of the individual, and delivering health in a way that makes the best use of the resources available. Different frameworks have approached categorising people-centred health systems in diverse – though ultimately complementary – ways, including through the role of the person in people-centred health systems, the principles underlying people-centred systems, and how health systems must be organised to deliver people-centred care.

The European Observatory of Health Systems and Policies of WHO Europe has developed a broad framework identifying the three core roles people take in the health system, and how these interact with and influence care: voice, choice, and co-production. *Voice* refers to the service user as a citizen: they should be involved in health service and systems development and policies, from the micro-level (for example, community participation in service development and design), to the macro-level (taking people's voices into account by listening to their views and experiences and responding accordingly). Choice relates to the service user as a consumer: they are able to choose payers, providers, and treatments. Co-production denotes the role of the person as a participant in their own health: as a co-producer, through self-management and co-ordination, as well as through their role in shared decision-making and choosing treatments (Nolte, Merkur and Anell, 2020[3]). The idea of co-production moves away from the traditional view of the health system as one that that provides care as a "product" made for and delivered to patients, towards a view of health services continually shaped and reshaped by both, together.

Other frameworks are structured more around the principles of people-centred care than the roles of the service user in it. In the United Kingdom, the Health Foundation has developed a framework around the four guiding principles of people-centred care: personalisation, co-ordination, enablement, and dignity, respect, and compassion (Health Foundation., 2016[1]). Under this framework, people should be expected to receive personalised and co-ordinated care, support or treatment, through a health system that enables them to identify and build their personal abilities and strengths, facilitating a more autonomous and satisfying life.

A third approach takes a 'roadmap' approach to what must be in place to achieve people-centredness, focusing on structure, process, and outcome (Santana et al., 2018[2]). At the systems or organisational level, it is critical to facilitate a culture of person-centred care, including co-designing educational programmes, health promotion and prevention programmes, enabling the workforce commitment to person-centred care, developing structures that facilitate good use of health information technology, and develop structures that help to measure and monitor person-centred care (Santana et al., 2018[5]). This forms the structure that enables person-centred care. Cultivating communication, respectful and compassionate care, engaging patients in their care, and integrating care underpin the process by which person-centred care is then delivered. Lastly, to demonstrate the value of person-centred care and ensure that it lives up to its intentions, it is critical that relevant outcomes, including access to care and patient-recorded outcomes, are measured.

In addition to the framework in development by WHO Europe mentioned above, the World Health Organization also published in 2016 an analysis that takes a 'roadmap' approach: the Framework on Integrated People-centred Health Services (World Health Organization Regional Office for Europe, 2016[4]). With strong emphasis on the notion of integration of services, the framework proposes five strategies to achieve a vision of people-centred health systems: (1) engaging and empowering people and communities; (2) strengthening governance and accountability; (3) reorienting the model of care; (4) co-ordinating services within and across sectors; and (5) creating an enabling environment.

While existing frameworks for people-centred care propose different structures for thinking about this concept, they share many of the same underlying principles for what key principles must be put in place to move towards a people-centred health system. The OECD Framework for People-Centred Health Systems builds on this previous work to further refine the key dimensions of people-centred health systems and the health systems policies that must be in place to achieve people-centredness. It is intended to work in parallel, and not replace other frameworks developed by the OECD, such as the OECD Framework for Health System Performance Measurement, originally developed in 2006 (Kelley and Hurst, 2006[6]) and revised in 2015 (OECD Health Care Quality Indicators Expert Group, 2015[7]).

The OECD Framework on People-Centred Health Systems takes further the key building blocks identified as foundational to achieving people-centredness. It identifies five dimensions of people-centred care from the literature – including ensuring voice, choice, co-production, respectfulness, and integration – and provides key quantitative indicators for domains and policy benchmarks that can help countries assess to what extent their systems are people-centred. By underpinning the key priorities of people-centred systems with key outcome, process and policy measures, the framework also helps to identify synergies to make health systems more people-centred. The dimensions, domains and policy benchmarks for the OECD Framework for People-Centred health Systems are presented in Table 1.1 below.

Table 1.1. Dimensions, domains and policy benchmarks for the OECD Framework for People Centred-Health Systems

Dimensions	Domains and policy benchmarks
Voice	People having a formal role in in health policy decision-making bodies or processes
Choice	People have a choice of health care providers
	People do not face barriers to access
Co-production	People are given accessible information during care
	People are consulted about their care
	People are engaged in their care
	People use digital tools to engage with their health and with the health system
Integration	Digital technology is used for integration of care
	Electronic clinical records are used
	People experience integration and co-ordinated care
Respectfulness	People receive high personal attention during care
	People feel treatment is fair
	People are treated with respect by health care professionals

How people-centred are OECD health systems? The OECD Scorecard for People-Centred Health Systems

In recent years, as countries have moved towards developing more people-centred health systems and services, a range of frameworks and definitions have attempted to capture what components are most necessary in transforming existing systems. While there have been growing efforts to capture patient voice through the development and implementation of patient-reported measures, there have not been similar efforts to benchmark the extent to which health systems as a whole are delivering people-centred care. Initiatives to strengthen patient-reported measures, including the OECD Patient-Reported Indicators Surveys (PaRIS), are critical to understanding people-centredness, but reflect only part of the story of whether health systems as a whole are performing in a people-centred way. Healthcare governance, physical and financing structures, training, incentives, and many other levers can influence whether people are able to receive person-centred care.

To help countries to assess the progress they are making towards people-centred care, and identify whether there are certain dimensions or policy areas that could benefit from particular attention, a Scorecard was developed for this report. It identifies policy benchmarks across the five dimensions of the OECD People-Centred Health Systems Framework. Thirteen policy indicators were selected for inclusion in the Scorecard (Table 1.2). The benchmarks included in the Scorecard were selected based on their policy relevance to each dimension. They also take into account considerable challenges related to data availability across countries. An evaluation of available data conducted for this report strongly indicates that **good data to assess people-centred health systems remains the exception rather than the rule**. Regularly collecting data across the key dimensions that make up a people-centred system will be critical to effect a transformation towards people-centredness across all levels of care.

Table 1.2. Scorecard indicators

Dimension	Policy benchmarks
Voice	Participation in decision-making bodies: Patients having a formal participation role in health policy
Choice	Choice of health care providers: Patient choice for primary, specialist and hospital care
	Access to health care: Unmet need due to affordability
Co-production	Patients given accessible information: Share of patients receiving easy-to-understand explanations by their doctor
	Patients are consulted about their care: Share of patients being informed or consulted about their care
	Share of individuals using digital tools for health: Proportion of patients using patient portals and apps
	Patients are engaged in their care: Share of individuals using the internet for seeking health information in the previous 3 months
Integration	Use of digital technology for integration of care: Computers used by primary care physician for common tasks
	Use of electronic clinical records: Share of primary care physician offices using Electronic Clinical Records
	Co-ordination of care: Share of patients not experiencing a problem with care co-ordination
Respectfulness	High personal attention: Share of patients who spent enough time with their regular doctor or any doctor during the consultation
	Fair treatment: Share of people agreeing that people are treated equally in their area
	Respectful treatment: Share of hospital patients treated by doctors and nurses with respect

The indicators included in the scorecard draw on a range of data sources, including OECD Health Statistics, the European Quality of Life Surveys, and the Commonwealth Fund International Health Policy Surveys. Measures were selected based on their relevance to the underlying dimension of the OECD framework, the robustness of the indicator, data availability, and comparability across countries. While the choice of dimensions was based on a thorough literature review, the choice of indicators was also further influenced by the availability of data. The choice of indicators also reflects a compromise between pertinence to the concept of people-centredness and availability of internationally comparable data. Individual countries may have additional indicators that could further contextualise an analysis of person-centredness in their health system that are not widely internationally comparable, and so excluded from this analysis. The full development of the *PaRIS International Survey of People Living with Chronic Conditions* will help to improve the availability of indicators, both within countries and internationally.

A measure of a country's performance on each dimension was taken based on the scorecard indicators, with countries grouped together in the top-, middle-, and lowest-performing third for each indicator. Because the indicators capture different aspects of the dimensions, and because the relationship between different dimensions of person-centredness are complex, no comprehensive 'ranking' of countries based on their overall performance across the scorecard was taken. Results of the benchmarking exercise suggest that while countries have made progress towards developing people-centred health systems, no country performs strongly across all dimensions. All countries have room to take further steps towards putting people at the centre of their health systems.

Table 1.3. A People-Centred Health Systems Scorecard: Key indicators of health systems' voice, choice, co-production, integrated care, and respectful care

	Voice	Choice		Co-production				Integrated care			Respectful care		
	Participation in decision-making bodies	Choice of healthcare providers	Access to healthcare	Patients given accessible information	Patients are consulted about their care	Use of digital tools for patient engagement	People are engaged in their care	Use of digital technology for integration of care	Use of electronic clinical records	Coordination of care	High personal attention	Respectful treatment	Fair treatment
	Patients having a formal participation role in health policy	Patients being able to choose providers in: primary, specialist, or hospital care	Population foregoing care because of affordability	Share of patients receiving easy-to-understand explanations by a doctor	Share of patients being involved in decisions about their care	Share of individuals using patient portals and apps	Share of individuals using the internet for seeking health information in the previous 3 months	Computers used by primary care physicians in prescriptions, referrals, and orders	Share of primary care physician offices using Electronic Clinical Records	Share of patients not experiencing a problem with care coordination	Share of patients who spent enough time with their regular doctor or any doctor during the consultation	People are treated with respect by doctors and nurses in hospital	Share of people agreeing that people are treated equally in their area
Australia	3	3	..	93.1	91.2	17.6	42.5	3	96.2	71.7	87.3	83.8	..
Austria	2	3	9.9	..	..	..	56.3	3	80.0	..	..	..	76.3
Belgium	2	3	..	97.7	..	..	51.0	..	..	..	97.5	..	58.4
Canada	2	1	..	91.2	84.8	18.7	..	1	77.2	75.3	82.4	84.8	..
Chile	2	1	..	..	..	..	..	3	65.0	..	..	..	..
Colombia							40.8						
Czech Republic	1	3	6.1	96.3	81.7	..	62.1	1	77.6	..	..	..	51.3
Denmark	1	2	19.9	..	..	..	72.1	3	100.0	..	..	..	87.3
Estonia	2	3	31.7	84.2	78.3	..	58.2	3	99.0	..	83.6	..	73.7
Finland	1	1	20.1	..	..	..	77.2	3	100.0	..	..	..	67.0
France	2	3	..	91.1	74.1	39.7	49.6	1	80.0	66.5	83.5	94.1	68.1
Germany	3	3	13.4	93.7	88.6	14.6	70.1	3	..	59.7	86.9	89.6	60.1
Greece	2	3	25.6	..	80.1	..	52.0	3	100.0	..	..	..	42.3
Hungary	1	..	13.9	93.1	..	..	63.0	..	..	..	87.5	..	..
Iceland	1	2	20.9	..	..	..	68.6	2	100.0	..	..	..	..
Ireland	2	3	34.4	95.9	89.8	..	59.9	3	95.0	..	..	..	72.0
Israel	2	2	..	..	..	..	50.0	3	100.0	..	93.9	..	..
Italy	1	2	16.9	94.2	..	..	35.0	2	..	..	..	..	48.0
Japan	..	3	..	..	..	..	..	..	..	..	42.1	..	..
Korea	..	..	..	82.9	82.4	..	67.6	..	..	..	80.8	..	..
Latvia	1	3	34.7	..	..	..	49.2	1	70.0	..	..	..	..

	Voice	Choice		Co-production				Integrated care			Respectful care		
	Participation in decision-making bodies	Choice of healthcare providers	Access to healthcare	Patients given accessible information	Patients are consulted about their care	Use of digital tools for patient engagement	People are engaged in their care	Use of digital technology for integration of care	Use of electronic clinical records	Coordination of care	High personal attention	Respectful treatment	Fair treatment
	Patients having a formal participation role in health policy	Patients being able to choose providers in: primary, specialist, or hospital care	Population foregoing care because of affordability	Share of patients receiving easy-to-understand explanations by a doctor	Share of patients being involved in decisions about their care	Share of individuals using patient portals and apps	Share of individuals using the internet for seeking health information in the previous 3 months	Computers used by primary care physicians in prescriptions, referrals, and orders	Share of primary care physician offices using Electronic Clinical Records	Share of patients not experiencing a problem with care coordination	Share of patients who spent enough time with their regular doctor or any doctor during the consultation	People are treated with respect by doctors and nurses in hospital	Share of people agreeing that people are treated equally in their area
Lithuania	..	1	8.9	..	..	..	57.1	..	..	..	..		62.9
Luxembourg	2	3	16.1	97.5	95.6	..	53.0	1	..	..	95.5		72.1
Mexico		1	..				49.8						
Netherlands	2	3	5.7	94.1	88.4	22.1	76.2	3	..	76.6	91.1	90.7	71.7
New Zealand	..	..	..	92.8	89.6	32.4	..	3	..	78.6	86.2	93.4	..
Norway	1	3	6.5	90.1	86.7	57.2	73.5	3	100.0	55.8	81.6	90.3	..
Poland	2	3	17.2	79.0	61.5	..	42.8	..	30.0	..	70.0		59.8
Portugal	3	1	28.6	96.3	90.9	..	49.0	3	..	..	89.7		58.9
Slovak Republic	..	..	7.4	..	..	..	56.0	..	89.0	..	..		46.2
Slovenia	1	3	15.6	..	..	..	57.9	2	..	..	..		51.4
Spain	2	1	17.4	..	78.0	..	67.1	3	99.0	..	..		56.9
Sweden	..	3	..	81.9	81.2	49.2	67.3	3	100.0	70.5	69.0	92.9	70.3
Switzerland	2	3	..	92.0	86.9	10.1	66.9	2	40.0	78.0	86.3	88.8	..
Turkey	1	3	..	..	..	..	50.8	2	..	..	..		51.5
United Kingdom	2	2	6.5	86.7	88.9	19.7	63.3	3	99.0	66.1	72.7	76.5	65.9
United States	..		..	92.1	89.8	57.5	38.3	3	83.0	78.8	83.5	88.9	..
Valid n	27	31	22	21	20	11	33	25	22	11	20	11	22
Average	1.8	2.4	17.2	91.2	84.4	30.8	57.4	2.4	85.5	70.7	82.5	88.5	62.4

Source: 1. OECD Health System Characteristics Survey 2016. 2. OECD Health Statistics 2019, OECD Health Care Quality Indicators. 3. OECD Information and Communication Technology Statistics 2019, OECD ICT Access and Usage by Households and Individuals. 4. OECD HCQI Survey of Electronic Health Record System Development and Use, 2016. 5. Commonwealth Fund International Health Policy Survey 2016. 6. European Quality of Life Survey 2016.

An analysis of key policy benchmarks

Voice: designing health care and the future of health services together with people, families and communities

The dimension of *voice* captures the importance of involving people who use the health system – as well as their families and communities – in macro, or systems-level decision making processes. The ability to make decisions and influence the care they receive is critical to a health system centred on the people who use it. It will be essential to ensure that people are involved in decisions about their health care, from the individual to the systems level. Capturing the extent to which patient voices are in institutionalised in macro decision-making processes – across different levels and areas of the health system – is important to understanding the weight which is given to users of the health system in designing the system.

As part of the benchmarking exercise, a composite indicator that captures the institutionalisation of patient voices in decision-making processes across different areas of the health system was developed, using information from the 2016 OECD Health Systems Characteristics Survey (Box 1.1). The indicator identifies the extent to which patients have a formal role in health policy making by assessing whether patients have a formal role in: (1) licensing of pharmaceuticals, (2) coverage or reimbursement, (3) health technology assessment, (4) decisions related to service planning, and (5) definition of public health objectives. Countries were scored on a 1-3 scale depending on the number of areas in which patients have a formal role: countries with a formal role in none or one area were assigned a score of one, countries with formal roles in two or three areas were assigned a score of two, and countries with four or five areas were assigned a score of three.

Box 1.1. Voice

Patient representatives: Patients have a formal role in health policy

- **Rationale:** Captures the institutionalisation of patient voices in decision-making processes across different areas of the health system.
- **Construction of the indicator:** A composite measure based on country responses to five questions, assessing whether patients have a formal role in: (1) licensing of pharmaceuticals, (2) coverage or reimbursement, (3) health technology assessment, (4) decisions related to service planning, and (5) definition of public health objectives. Countries are scored on a 1-3 scale depending on the number of areas in which patients have a formal role: countries with a formal role in none or one area were assigned a score of one, countries with formal roles in two or three areas were assigned a score of two, and countries with four or five areas were assigned a score of three.
- **Data source:** OECD Health Systems Characteristics Survey, 2016
- **Country coverage:** 27 OECD countries

Results of the benchmarking exercise (Figure 1.1) indicate that few countries have systematically included patients across all areas of health policy decision-making, with one-third of reporting countries indicating that patients play almost no formal role. Only three countries – **Australia**, **Germany**, and **Portugal** – systematically include patients in at least four areas of health policy making. Involving patients in decision-making processes is important to ensuring that health systems and services are designed to best meet people's needs – in other words, to ensure health care is people-centred. Studies have shown that where input from patients or other community members is included in health initiatives, outcomes related to social impact – beyond the impact on health – are more likely to be captured and reported (Hoon Chuah et al., 2018[8]).

At the same time, official patient involvement in decision-making bodies should be considered a necessary but not sufficient component of a person-centred health systems approach. Even where patients or public representatives may be involved in decision-making, there remains continued debate over what effective public involvement means and looks like (Rozmovits et al., 2018[9]). Experts have called on decision makers to carefully consider the ethical challenges of designing high-quality patient involvement, including the ethics of patient selection and the frequent power imbalance between patient participants and other members of decision-making groups such as health technology assessments (HTA) (Vanstone et al., 2019[10]). In **Australia**, interviews with stakeholders involved in HTA and health funding decisions demonstrated a lack of consensus between representatives of patient organisations and other stakeholders in the adequacy of existing processes and what should be considered as evidence to guide decision making, with patient representatives more likely to consider broader social and emotional factors beyond bioclinical outcomes ((Lopes, Carter and Street, 2015[11]; Lopes et al., 2016[12]). Similar tensions around the conceptualisation of evidence were found in a review of assessments for cancer drug reviews in Canada (Rozmovits et al., 2018[9]).

Figure 1.1. Institutionalisation of patients in decision-making

Number of areas of health policy making where patients are formally included (maximum = 5)

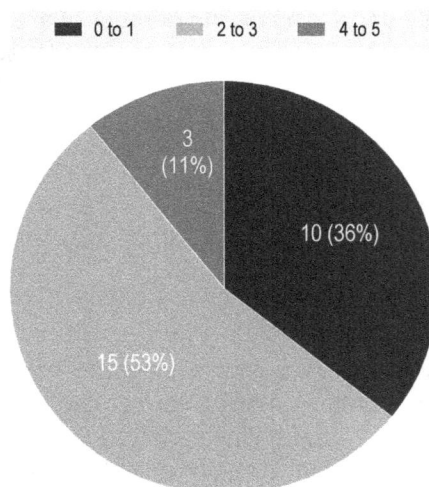

Note: Assesses whether patients have a formal role in: (1) licensing of pharmaceuticals, (2) coverage or reimbursement, (3) health technology assessment, (4) decisions related to service planning, and (5) definition of public health objectives.
Source: OECD (2016[13]), Health Systems Characteristics Survey.

Patient voice is not included evenly across areas of health policy decision-making: just over one-third (35%) of countries reported that a patient or citizen representative is included in decision-making around the licensing of pharmaceuticals, compared with nearly three-fifths (57%) that reported patients or citizen representatives are involved in coverage or reimbursement decisions.

Figure 1.2. Patient or citizen representative included in decision-making

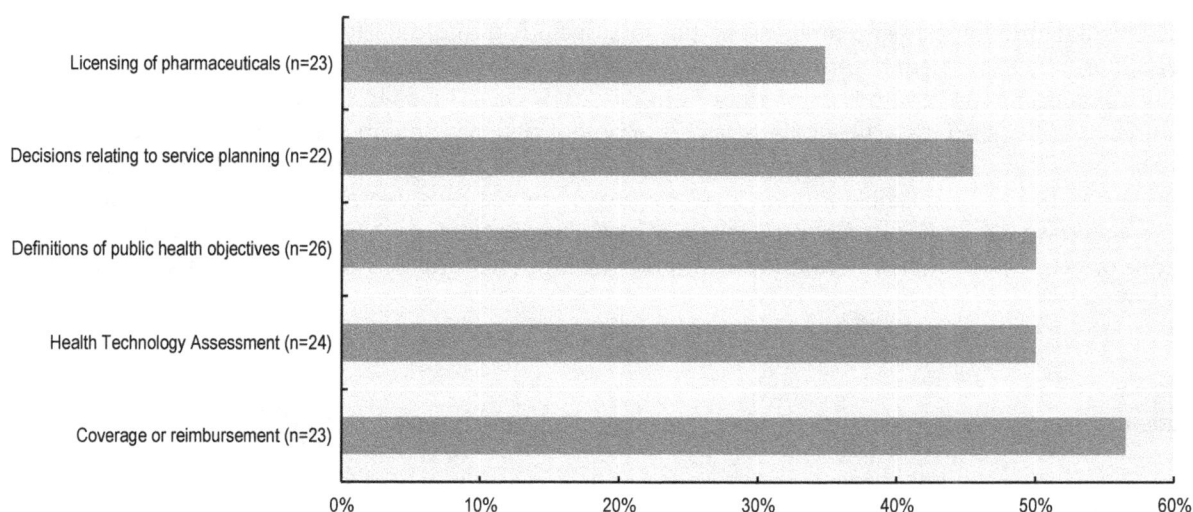

Source: OECD (2016[13]), Health Systems Characteristics Survey.

During the COVID-19 pandemic, the speed at which decisions were made – particularly at the beginning of the pandemic – meant that patient voices were often excluded from decision making processes (Richards and Scowcroft, 2020[14]). Evidence from COVID-19 task forces across 24 countries suggests that not only were patients largely excluded from decision making, but that response efforts were largely concentrated among politicians, virologists and epidemiologists, with less input from frontline workers, civil society and social policy experts (Rajan et al., 2020[15]). Ensuring any public health response is person-centred must anticipate the way that policies will affect all populations – particularly responses that so drastically upend the social fabric and daily lives of much of the population. A failure to include patients in consultation and decision making – and a failure to consider the diverse backgrounds of people more broadly – will make it more difficult to anticipate the impacts that rapidly developed containment policies will have on different groups of people in society.

Including patients proactively in health emergency and pandemic response structures could help to ensure patient and family voices are not lost during health shocks. In Ontario, Canada, the Kingston Health Sciences Centre, a university hospital, included patient advisors in scenario planning before pandemic restrictions were imposed, and ensured the chair of the Patient and Family Advisory Council was a full member of the Incident Command team responsible for changing services during the pandemic. Input from patients and family members were directly responsible for certain policy changes implemented during the pandemic, including policies around in-person family visits (Bardon, 2021[16]).

Choice: making systems more responsive to people's needs and preferences

Individuals are consumers of health services and goods, and increasingly wish to have a say in which goods and services they choose, and how. This dimension recognises the importance of providing care that meets people's expectations, including providing multiple options and alternatives to how care is delivered, to ensure it best meets their needs. At its most straightforward, patients can be given literal choice in the health care services they seek out – for example, choice of physician or hospital. In some cases, this choice is unencumbered, with no gatekeepers, incentives, or other barriers. Even beyond the policy barriers put in place, however, other factors – such as affordability and geography – can create limitations to the ability of patients to exercise the choice they have on paper (OECD, 2019[17]).

The measures of choice included in the OECD benchmarking exercise were selected to measure two components of choice: what is available according to the health system policies of a country, and the level of access patients have based on extrinsic barriers, including affordability (Box 1.2). To evaluate patient choice throughout the health care system, a composite measure based on choice in primary, specialist, and hospital care was created, using data from the 2016 OECD Health Systems Characteristic Survey. Countries were scored on a 1-3 scale based on whether patients have a choice in their selection of their primary care physician, specialist care services, and hospital services. Where the choice of providers is not possible, or is only possible for one level of care, countries received a score of one. Countries where choice was possible on two of the three levels of care (irrespective of which levels these were) were given a score of two, while those where choice was reported possible across all three levels were assigned a score of three.

Box 1.2. Choice

Patients can choose providers in: primary care, specialist care, hospital care

- **Rationale:** Intended to evaluate patient choice throughout the health system – from primary to tertiary care.
- **Construction of the indicator:** A composite measure based on three questions, assessing whether patients have choice in their selection of (1) primary care physician, (2) specialist care services, and (3) hospital services. Countries are scored on a 1-3 scale. Countries where choice of providers is not possible or where it is possible for only one level of care were assigned a score of one, countries where choice if possible in two of three levels were assigned a score of two, and countries where choice is possible in all three levels of care were assigned a score of three.
- **Data source:** OECD Health Systems Characteristics Survey, 2016
- **Country coverage:** 31 OECD countries

Access: Patients who went without care because of affordability

- **Rationale:** Intended to evaluate the extent of cost barriers to access and choice in the health system
- **Construction of the indicator:** An aggregate measure based on an affirmative response to unmet need due to financial reasons for four types of health care services: medical needs, dental needs, mental health service needs, and prescription drug needs. Only respondents who reported having a health care need over the previous year were included.
- **Data source:** OECD Health at a Glance 2019, based on EHIS-2 statistics
- **Country coverage:** 22 OECD countries

Patient choice appears to be well institutionalised across a majority of OECD countries. More than half of OECD countries responding to the OECD Health Systems Characteristics Survey reported that patients were given free choice in their selection of primary, specialist, and hospital care, with fewer than 10% reporting that patients were strictly limited in their choice of care (Figure 1.3). A plurality of countries attempt to influence patient choice using financial incentives – particularly at the specialist and hospital levels – though patient choice is not fully circumscribed.

Figure 1.3. Patient choice in primary, specialist and hospital care

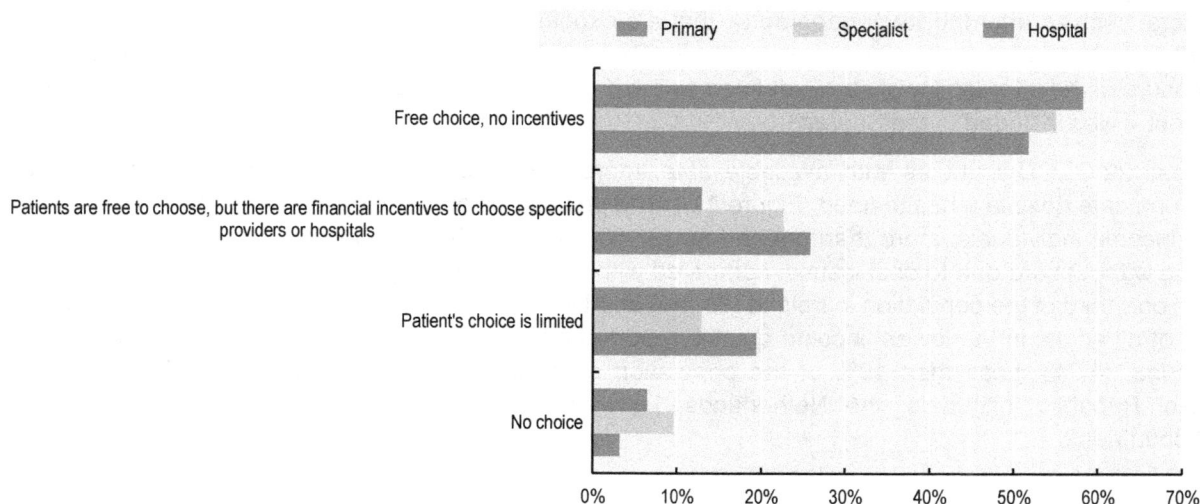

Note: For "no choice" at the primary and specialist levels, patients are assigned to a specific provider.
Source: OECD (2016[13]), Health Systems Characteristics Survey.

In half (16) of countries, primary care acts as some form of gatekeeper to specialist care – either through strictly requiring primary care referrals to access specialist care (9 countries), or through financial incentives (7 countries) for patients to receive a referral from their primary care physician for further specialist care (Figure 1.4).

Figure 1.4. Primary care control of specialist care

Proportion of countries reporting (of 32 countries)

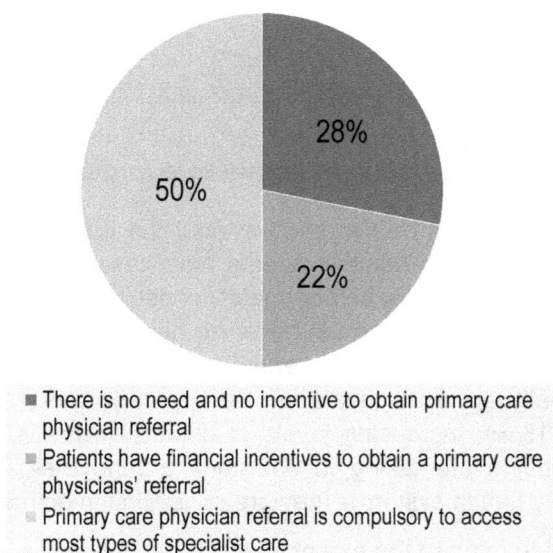

- There is no need and no incentive to obtain primary care physician referral
- Patients have financial incentives to obtain a primary care physicians' referral
- Primary care physician referral is compulsory to access most types of specialist care

1. Patients are able to directly access specialist care, despite the financial incentives. 2. Except in cases of emergency.
Source: OECD (2016[13]), Health Systems Characteristics Survey.

Beyond the institutional rules governing patient choice, the ability to choose health care – including selecting physicians or facilities, but also more basic questions of seeking care – is further influenced by factors, such as affordability or geography, that are exogenous to the direct rules of a health care system but can nevertheless impact access to services. To capture how choice may be constrained by access, a measure of the affordability of care – defined as the proportion of the population who had forgone care due to cost – was included in the Scorecard.

Across 22 OECD countries with available data, more than one in six adults (17.2%) reported having forgone care despite a health need (Figure 1.5). The prevalence of forgone care is particularly high among low-income individuals: more than one in four (27.5%) individuals in the lowest income quintile reported going without care due to cost issues, compared with just 8.9% among the highest income quintile. More than one-third of the population in Ireland (34.4%) and Latvia (34.7%) reported foregoing care, while nearly half of all adults in the lowest income quintile reported doing so in Estonia (46.9%), Latvia (55.2%), and Portugal (47%). Less than 10% of the population reported forgoing care in only seven (Austria, the Czech Republic, Lithuania, the Netherlands, Norway, the Slovak Republic, United Kingdom) of the 22 countries.

Figure 1.5. Population forgoing care because of affordability, 2014

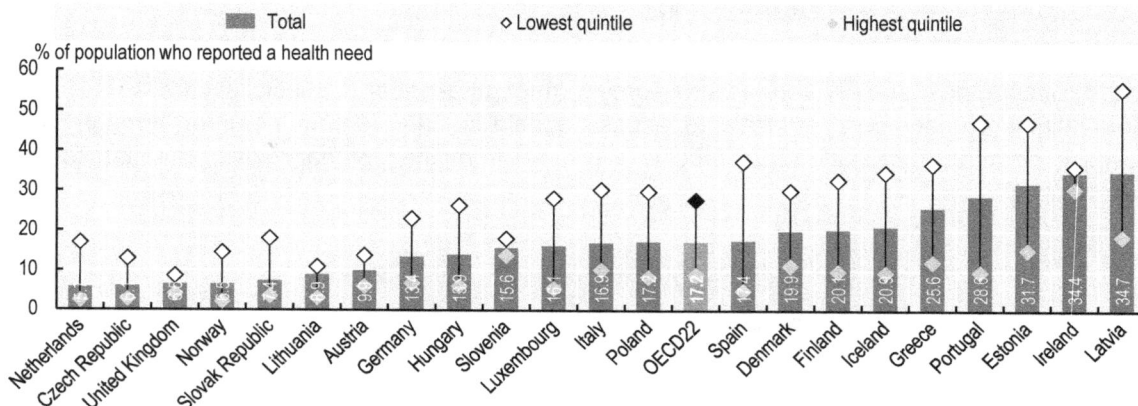

Source: OECD (2019[18]), *Health at a Glance 2019: OECD Indicators*, https://doi.org/10.1787/4dd50c09-en.

Co-production: enabling people to play an active role in decisions about their health

A people-centred health system cannot be designed without the participation of those who use it. Co-production captures the extent to which health systems have taken steps to involve people and local communities in their own care. Patients must be adequately consulted about their care, including receiving sufficient information from their doctors, and must have the health literacy and information they need to make decisions that are well-informed. Previous research has indicated that despite a growing recognition of the need to improve health literacy, levels of literacy nevertheless remain low across many OECD countries (Moreira, 2018[19]). Increasing levels of health literacy is particularly critical given the growing ownership many patients are taking in decisions around their health, and new sources of information – often outside they health system – they are consulting in doing so (OECD, 2019[20]).

Four measures were identified to capture the extent to which patients are active participants in their care, as well as how much opportunity they feel they are given by the health system to do so (Box 1.3). Two measures evaluate the extent to which patients feel the health system offers them the ability to make decisions about their care. To evaluate whether patients feel they are consulted and given sufficient information to make informed decisions, a patient-reported measure of the share of patients receiving easy-to-understand explanations by their doctor was constructed, using data from the OECD Health Statistics (based on data from national sources and the Commonwealth Fund). A second measure, using the same sources, measures the patient experience in being involved as much as they wish to be in decisions about their care and treatment.

In addition to the variables that evaluate the degree to which the health system – through its doctors and medical staff – give patients the tools and opportunities they need to make informed decisions about their health, two further variables were included that consider how patients avail themselves of information. Using information from the OECD Information and Communication Technology Statistics, a measure of how patients seek information from general sources was included based on the share of individuals who reported seeking health information on the internet during the previous three months. A further measure capturing patient engagement with tools developed by health systems, based on data from the Commonwealth Fund, was also included for a more limited set of countries.

Box 1.3. Co-production

Share of patients receiving easy-to-understand explanations by their doctor

- **Rationale**: Patients are able to make informed decisions about their care, because they are consulted and given sufficient information to do so.
- **Construction of the indicator:** A patient-reported measure adjusted for age and sex, based on the question, "When you need care or treatment, how often does the doctor or medical staff you see explain things in a way that is easy to understand". Respondents who answered "always" or "often" were categorised as a yes. Respondents who answered "sometimes" or "rarely or never" were categorised as a "no".
- **Data source:** OECD Health Statistics and 2020 Commonwealth Fund International Health Policy Survey
- **Country coverage:** 21 OECD countries

Share of patients involved in decisions about their care

- **Rationale**: Patients are given an opportunity to be involved in decisions about their care.
- **Construction of the indicator:** A patient-reported measure, adjusted for age and sex on the question whether a doctor involved them as much as they wanted to be in decisions about their care and treatment. Answers were categorised as "Yes" or "No".
- **Data source:** OECD Health Statistics and 2020 Commonwealth Fund International Health Policy Survey
- **Country coverage:** 20 OECD countries

Share of individuals using digital tools for health care

- **Rationale**: Patients use digital health systems tools to engage actively in their own health and with the health system.
- **Construction of the indicator:** A patient-reported measure, adjusted for age and sex, based on the proportion of respondents who reported using secure websites, patient portals or apps on their mobile phones to communicate or email with their primary care practice and/or view online or download their health information, such as visit summaries, tests or laboratory results.
- **Data source:** 2020 Commonwealth Fund International Health Policy Survey
- **Country coverage:** 11 OECD countries

Share of individuals using the internet for seeking health information

- **Rationale**: Patients demonstrate they are engaged in their care by seeking information from both within and outside the health system.
- **Construction of the indicator:** Share of individuals using the internet for seeking health information in the previous 3 months (%) (self-reported)
- **Data source:** OECD Information and Communication Technology Statistics, 2020 (or nearest year)
- **Country coverage:** 33 OECD countries

Results indicate that patients report being largely satisfied with the accessibility of information they are given by their doctors, and broadly feel included in decisions about their care. On average across 17 OECD countries, more than nine in ten (91.2%) respondents reported feeling that they received easy-to-understand explanations by their doctor, while more than four in five (84.4%) reported being involved with their doctor in decisions about their care. Fewer than 80% of respondents felt involved in their care in four countries (Estonia, France, Poland, Spain). The fewest respondents reported receiving easy-to-access information and being involved in their care in Poland, where just under four in five (79%) respondents reported being given accessible information, and just over three in five (61.5%) reporting that they were consulted about their care. At least nine in ten patients reported both being given accessible information and involved in their care in five countries – Australia, Israel, Luxembourg, Portugal, and the United States.

Over the past decade, the proportion of people using the internet on a regular basis has increased dramatically, as has the frequency and intensity of internet usage. These trends are reflected in the proportion of adults (aged 16-74) reporting that they had recently used the internet to seek health information. Between 2010 and 2020, the share of individuals reporting that they had gone online for information about health increased by nearly 70% on average across OECD countries, from just over one-third of adults (34.1%) to nearly three in five (57.4%). In more than one in four (8/30) countries with available data, the proportion of adults using the internet for health information more than doubled between 2010 and 2020.

Health systems have invested significantly in scaling up patient-oriented digital health tools, including the development of patient portals and apps that offer patients direct access to their health data and information (often linked to electronic health records), the ability to communicate with health professionals, the ability to access prescriptions, and other tools. Previous analyses have suggested that uptake of many of these tools remained relatively low (OECD, 2019[20]). Data from the 2020 Commonwealth Fund International Health Policy Survey confirms that patient portal use is not yet widespread. On average across the 11 countries surveyed, just three in ten patients reported having used patient portals or apps to communicate with their doctors or download health information. Fewer than one in five patients reported using patient portals and apps for these purposes in nearly half of all reporting countries (Australia, Canada, Germany, Switzerland, United Kingdom). Norway, Sweden and the United States reported close to or more than half of respondents engaging with patient portals and apps to communicate with their doctors or download health information.

Nevertheless, while health-seeking behaviour has increased dramatically, a significant plurality of the population does not yet use the internet for health information purposes. Fewer than half of adults report using the internet for health information in eight (27%) countries, with just over one-third (35%) of adults in Italy having done so. In Finland, the country with the highest share of respondents using the internet for health information, just over three-quarters (77%) of adults reported having sought health information online within the previous three months. Individuals with higher levels of educational attainment, as well as younger adults, were more likely to have reported going online to seek out health information, compared with older and less highly educated adults. Among adults with high educational attainment, three-quarters (75%) reported having sought out health information online recently, compared with just over two in five (42%) adults with low educational attainment. These trends echo broader patterns of unequal access to new digital tools, and risk exacerbating existing inequalities affecting high-quality person-centred care, including around issues of choice (access to services) and co-production (health literacy) (OECD, 2019[20]).

The reduction in in-person consultations and health care services during the COVID-19 pandemic engendered a rapid rise in the adoption of teleconsultations and other digital health tools. On average across 22 European OECD countries, nearly half (45%) of respondents reported that they had used a teleconsultation service during the pandemic. Data from Israel, Norway and Australia suggest that in at least some cases, an uptick in the use of teleconsultation services replaced many of the in-person visits that were postponed or forgone due to the pandemic: In Israel, the number of teleconsultations per capita nearly doubled between 2019 and 2020, while in Norway teleconsultations per capita increased eightfold between 2019 and 2020 (OECD, 2021[21]).

Figure 1.6. Share of adults who received services from a doctor via telemedicine since the start of the pandemic, 2020 and 2021

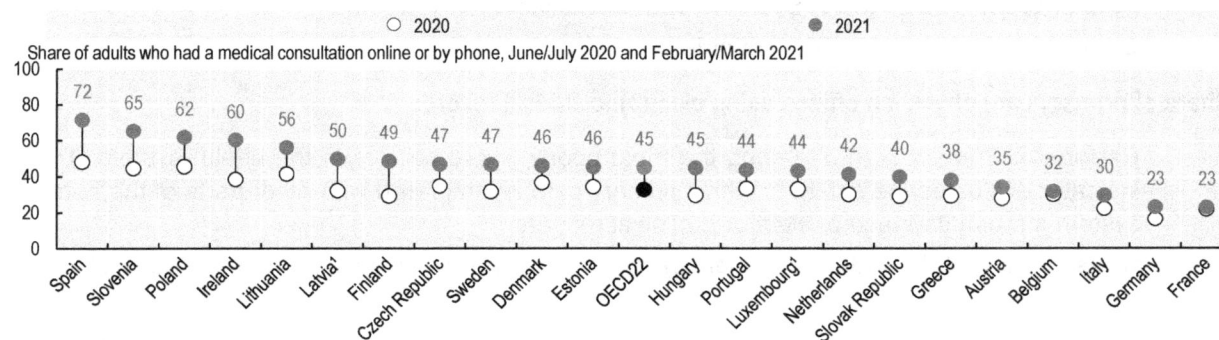

Note: Low reliability in one or both rounds.
Source: OECD (2021[21]), *Health at a Glance 2021: OECD Indicators*, https://doi.org/10.1787/ae3016b9-en.

Integration: co-ordinating care for and around the person in need

In addition to the implications of fragmentation on overall efficiency and outcomes, poor integration within the health system makes navigating care and services difficult for the people who need them. Better integrated care among patients with chronic conditions has been found to improve well-being and quality of life, while helping to improve self-management of care (Coulter et al., 2015[22]; Kruis et al., 2013[23]). Yet operations within the health system remain too fragmented, too often, with poor co-ordination of care around patients, and frequent fragmentation between health sectors, such as primary and hospital care.

To capture the extent to which health systems have the capacity to deliver integrated care to patients, three measures were identified for inclusion in the scorecard. Two concern the extent to which there has been progress in integrating primary health services – arguably the most critical node for co-ordinating care – with other parts of the health system, with the third measure reflecting the patient's views on the extent to which they have experienced problems with co-ordination after being discharged from hospital.

Box 1.4. Integration

Use of computers in primary care for tasks related to the integration of care

- **Rationale:** Primary care is among the most poorly linked sectors of the health system. This indicator evaluates the extent to which primary care services are electronically connected for the issuing of prescriptions, referrals, and orders in digital format.

- **Construction of the indicator:** A composite measure based on country responses to six questions. Each question refers to whether 75% or more of primary care physicians use computers to each of the following tasks: (1) making appointments, (2) ordering laboratory tests, (3) sending referral letters to specialists, (4) issuing drug prescriptions, (5) receiving alerts or prompts about drug dose or drug interaction, and (6) sending prescriptions to pharmacy. Countries are scored on a 1-3 scale depending on the number of areas in which primary care practitioners use a computer. In an attempt to establish three groups with a similar number of countries, countries with zero to four affirmative responses were given a score of one, countries with five affirmative responses were given a score of two, and countries with six affirmative responses were given a score of two.

- **Data source:** OECD Health Systems Characteristics Survey, 2016

- **Country coverage:** 25 OECD countries

Share of primary care physician offices using electronic clinical records

- **Rationale:** Primary care is among the most poorly linked sectors in the health system. This indicator evaluates the extent to which primary care is integrated with other parts of the health system through their use of electronic clinical records.

- **Construction of the indicator:** Share of primary care physician offices using electronic clinical records (%).

- **Data source:** OECD HCQI Survey of Electronic Health Record System Development and Use, 2016

- **Country coverage:** 22 OECD countries

Share of patients who have not experienced good care co-ordination

- **Rationale:** Beyond arguments for efficiency, care co-ordination and integration cannot be seen to be working if they are not felt by the people whose care is supposedly being integrated.

- **Construction of the indicator:** Among patients hospitalised at least once overnight over the previous two years, a patient-reported measure adjusted for age and sex, based on affirmative answers to both of two questions: (1) "When you left the hospital, did the hospital make arrangements or make sure you had follow-up care with a doctor or other health care professional?" and (2) "After you left the hospital, did the doctors or staff at the place where you usually get medical care seem informed and up-to-date about the care you received in the hospital?"

- **Data source:** Commonwealth Fund International Health Policy Survey, 2020

- **Country coverage:** 11 OECD countries

Primary care is a central node for delivering co-ordinated, person-centred care, and digital tools are a critical and promising tool to help overcome fragmentation between primary care and other parts of the health system. Yet despite this potential, and the broader scale-up of digital tools in health care, primary care has remained one of the most poorly linked sectors within the health system. While uptake of new digital tools has sometimes been slower in primary care, the majority of countries (15/25) reported that at least three-quarters of primary care physicians use computers to complete all identified tasks, including making appointments, issuing prescriptions, ordering laboratory tests, sending referrals, sending prescriptions to pharmacies, and being alerted of drug dose or drug interaction issues.

Figure 1.7. Computer use by primary care physicians

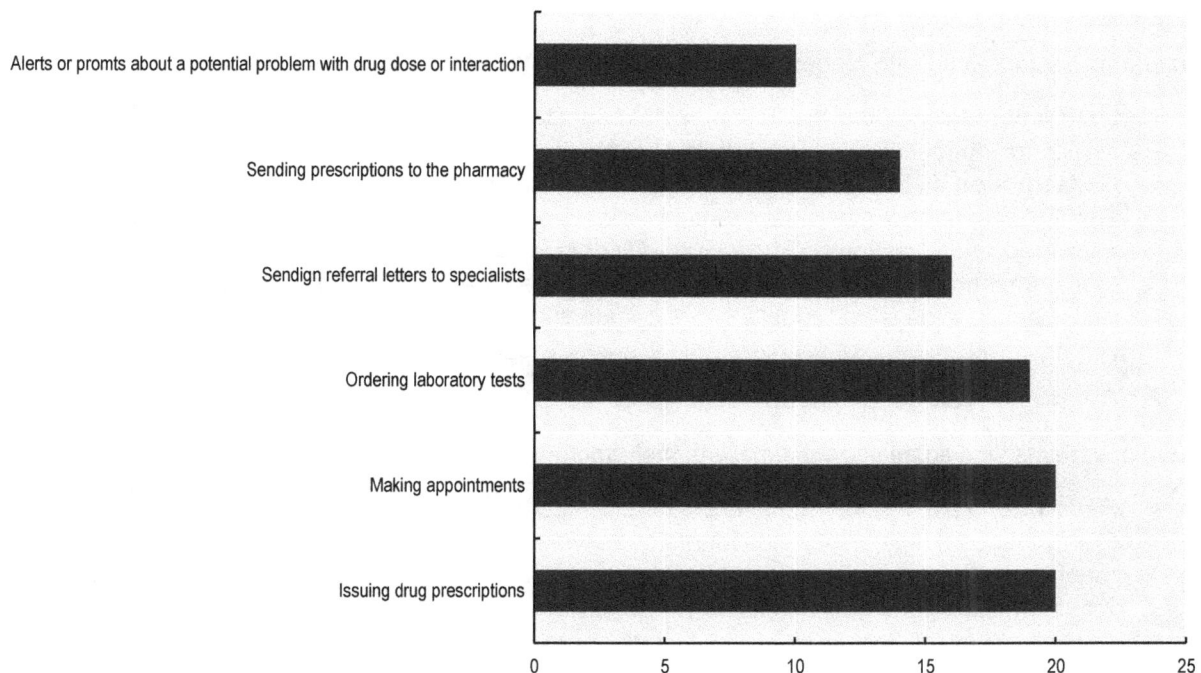

Source: OECD (2016[13]), Health Systems Characteristics Survey.

Encouragingly, the proportion of primary care physician offices who report using electronic clinical records in their practices has increased dramatically in recent years. The proportion of primary care offices using electronic clinical records increased from 70% in 2012 to 93% in 2021 (OECD, 2019[18]). More than 60% of responding countries reported that 90% or more primary care physician offices used electronic records in 2021, up from less than half in 2012.

In addition to having primary care serve as an important co-ordinating node for care management – particularly for patients with chronic conditions, ensuring a strong continuity of care as patients transition between sectors of the health systems is also important to ensuring health systems are well integrated. In a survey of hospitalised patients across 11 countries, nearly one in three (29%) reported that they had experienced problems with co-ordination of care when they left the hospital – either poor follow-up care arrangements from the hospital, or that their regular doctors did not appear to be informed and up to date about their care – including at least one in five patients in every responding country. That a large plurality of patients did not experience good follow-up upon hospital discharge is particularly concerning because poor or delayed follow-up care following a hospital admission has been associated with worse outcomes and an increased risk of hospital readmission, as well as poorer patient satisfaction (Jackson et al., 2015[24]; Braun et al., 2009[25]; Jack et al., 2009[26]). Many health systems have identified improving co-ordination of care between hospitals and the community as an important policy priority.

Respectfulness: treating patients with dignity

Compassion and respect are fundamental bedrocks of building a people-centred health system. Making sure that people are treated fairly and with respect, have their voices heard, and needs attended to, must be made the basic standard that people experience in their interactions throughout the health system.

Box 1.5. Respectfulness

Share of patients treated with respect by both doctors and nurses during a hospital stay

- **Rationale:** Making sure the patient feels respected by health care workers forms the basis for respectful interactions with the health care system.
- **Construction of the indicator:** An aggregate patient-reported measure, adjusted for age and sex, for patients hospitalised overnight at least once in the previous two years. Respondents answered two questions of how often (1) doctors and (2) nurses treated them with respect during their hospital stay. Respondents who reported that *both* doctors and nurses treated them with respect "always" or "usually" were categorised as having received respectful care.
- **Data source:** Commonwealth Fund International Health Policy Survey 2020
- **Country coverage:** 11 OECD countries

Share of patients who spent enough time with their doctor during the consultation

- **Rationale:** Making sure the patient is heard, that the consultation is thorough, and their care is tailored accordingly, is foundational to delivering truly person-centred care. This patient-reported measures captures the extent to which patients feel the physician spent enough time with them during the consultation.
- **Construction of the indicator:** A patient-reported measure, adjusted for age and sex. Respondents answered a question whether a doctor spend enough time with them. Answers were categorised in either "Yes" or "No".
- **Data source:** Commonwealth Fund International Health Policy Survey 2020 and OECD Health Statistics, 2016 (or nearest year)
- **Country coverage:** 20 OECD countries

Share of people agreeing that people are treated equally in their area

- **Rationale:** Equal treatment or lack of discrimination is also a sign of respectful care.
- **Construction of the indicator:** A patient-reported measure, based on the question, "To what extent do you agree or disagree with the following about GP, family doctor or health centre services in your area: All people are treated equally in these services in my area." Respondents who answered 7 or above were categorised as a "yes".
- **Data source:** European Quality of Life Survey 2016
- **Country coverage:** 22 OECD countries that are EU member countries

---

Encouragingly, nearly nine in ten patients (89%) across 11 OECD countries surveyed by the Commonwealth Foundation report feeling that both doctors and nurses treated them with respect during a recent hospital stay, ranging from just over three-quarters of patients in the United Kingdom to nearly 95% in France. Nearly as many (83%) across 20 OECD countries reported being satisfied with the level of attention given to them by their regular physician in primary care, reporting that their regular doctor spent enough time with them during their consultation. A relatively high proportion of respondents in a number of countries reported insufficient time spent with their regular doctor: In Japan, nearly three-fifths of respondents felt their doctors did not spend enough time with them, while about three in ten patients felt similar in Poland, Sweden and the United Kingdom.

While patients reported a relatively high level of satisfaction at the level of respectfulness they usually experience within the health system, there is substantially less trust in whether the health system treats others fairly. When asked whether the they agreed that people in their area are treated equally, an average of just over three-fifths of respondents across 22 OECD countries responded affirmatively, including close to half or fewer in the Czech Republic, Greece, Italy and the Slovak Republic.

The relevance of indicators of the OECD Scorecard for People-Centred Health Systems: a person-level analysis

Despite the broad agreement among OECD countries about the importance of people-centredness, empirical evidence on the association of the dimensions of people-centredness and people's perception of higher performance of the health system can strengthen the support for policy case even further. Therefore, an empirical exercise was conducted to examine whether people who had a better experience of the dimensions of the OECD Scorecard for People-Centred Health Systems were also more likely to agree that their health system performs better. This analysis may provide indication that people who have a better experience of voice, choice, co-production, integration, and respectfulness are more likely to agree that the performance of their health system is strong.

The policy question was examined with the help of a person-level dataset collected and published by Commonwealth Fund within its ongoing series of International Health Policy Survey (known as IHP survey). The IHP survey dataset used for the empirical analysis contains information from 22 961 adult health care users in 11 OECD countries (Australia, Canada, France, Germany, the Netherlands, New Zealand, Norway, Sweden, Switzerland, United Kingdom, United States), who answered questions related to their experiences with care and the health system in the first semester of 2020.

As indicated in the description of the 13 indicators of the OECD Scorecard presented in the previous sections, the IHP survey served as the primary source of data (i.e. for all countries) for the construction of 4 out of 13 indicators, namely "use of patient portals and apps", "patients do not experience a problem with co-ordination", "patients are treated with respect", "doctors spent enough time with patients"; and as a secondary source of data (i.e. for some countries) for other 2 indicators, namely "doctors provide easy to understand explanations", and "patients are involved in decision-making". Moreover, the IHP survey contains similar data to one more indicator, which is the absence of financial barriers of access to consultations. As such, the IHP survey has data covering the dimensions of choice, co-production, integration, and respectfulness of the OECD Framework for People-Centred health Systems. The only dimension of the OECD Framework for which person-level data was not available in the IHP survey is voice, which tends to be a system-level characteristic, for example when national policy includes patients in formal committees for decision making about the health system.

The empirical analysis confirmed that people who experienced higher levels of choice, co-production, integration of care, and respectfulness of care were more likely to agree that their health system performs well, even when gender, self-rated health status, and income level are taken into account. The methods used in the analysis are described in Box 1.6.

Box 1.6. Methods

For the analysis, data was retrieved by the 2020 round of the Commonwealth Fund IHP survey, conducted in 11 countries: Australia, Canada, France, Germany, the Netherlands, New Zealand, Norway, Sweden, Switzerland, United Kingdom, United States. The data contained information from 22 961 individuals, collected between February and May of 2020.

The Commonwealth Fund has explored the experiences of doctors and patients since 1998 through several surveys. These surveys foster opportunities for cross-national learning and health system improvement. The survey collects health-related data covering a broad range of topics – patient's access to care, the relationship with the doctor, patient's use and experience with specialists, experiences with care, health care coverage, experiences with prescribed medication, overall health, behaviour factors affecting health and social context, overall views of the health care system (Doty et al., 2021[27]).

In the analysis of this section, variables address topics related to dimensions of patient centred care systems emphasised in the OECD Framework for People-Centred Health Systems – *choice, co-production, integrated care,* and *respectful care.* A multivariate logistic regression was conducted in Stata 16.1 software to estimate the association of indicators in each of these dimensions and a dichotomous outcome variable for a strong performing health system. Given that poor self-rated health, income, and gender may influence the perception of health system performance, these control variables were included in the analysis. Country-level fixed effects were also included the average effects of the health system characteristic that affect respondents of each country.

The operationalisation of the indicators using in this analysis may differ somewhat from the ones presents in the scorecard for PCHS. However, the underlying concepts expressed by the variables in the present patient-level analysis and in the country-level scorecard are similar enough to ensure the validity of the exercise (Davis, Schoenbaum and Audet, 2005[28]). A definition of the variables in the regression model is presented in Box 1.7.

Given that two variables are only available for people who were hospitalised in the last two years (on integration, arrangements and information for follow-up care after hospitalisation were made, and on respectfulness, doctors and nurses treat patient with respect in hospital), two separate models were estimated, one including all people with complete data for all variables (3 289 observations) and another one including all people with complete data for all but the variables related to hospitalisation (18 269 observations). The results of the regression models are presented in Table 1.4.

Box 1.7. Questions Addressing Performance and Indicators of Dimensions of People-Centred Health Systems

Health system performance (outcome)

- "How would you rate the overall performance of the health care system in your country?". The answers "very good or good" were categorised as strong performance and coded as 1, while the answers "acceptable, poor or very poor" were coded as 0.

Choice

- During the past 12 months, was there a time when you had a medical problem but did not visit a doctor because of the cost?". Response categories are "yes" and "no". This question is transformed from using coding 1 for No and 0 for Yes to reflect a positive experience.

Co-Production

- "When you need care or treatment, how often does your regular doctor or medical staff you see explain things in a way that is easy to understand?" Response categories are divided in two categories; "often to always" was coded as 1 and "sometimes to rarely" was coded as 0.
- "When you need care or treatment, how often does your regular doctor or medical staff you see involve you as much as you want in decisions about your care and treatment?". Response categories are divided in two categories; "often to always" coded as 1 and "sometimes to rarely" coded as 0.
- "In the last two years, have you used a secure website or patient portal or an app on your mobile phone to communicate or email with your regular practice, or view online or downloaded your health information, such as visit summaries or your tests or laboratory results?". Response categories are 1 if at least one of these two actions was done, and 0 otherwise.

Integrated care

- "When you left the hospital, did the hospital make arrangements or make sure you had follow-up care with a doctor or other health care professional?" and "After you left the hospital, did the doctors or staff at the place where you usually get medical care seem informed and up-to-date about the care you received in the hospital?". This question is only available for patients who were hospitalised overnight at least once in the previous two years. Response categories are 1 if answers to both of these two actions was yes, 0 otherwise.

Respectful care

- "During this hospital stay, how often did doctors treat you with courtesy and respect?" and "During this hospital stay, how often did nurses treat you with courtesy and respect?". These questions are only available for patients who were hospitalised overnight at least once in the previous two years. Respondents who reported that *both* doctors and nurses treated them with respect "always or usually" were coded as 1, and 0 otherwise.
- "When you need care or treatment, how often does your regular doctor or medical staff you see spend enough time with you?". Response categories are divided in two categories; "often to always" was coded as 1 and "sometimes to rarely" was coded as 0.

Table 1.4. Dimensions of people-centredness and perception of high performance of the health system

Odds-ratio and confidence intervals calculated from multivariate logistic regressions

High performance of health system	Only those hospitalised in the past 2 years		All respondents	
	Odds ratio	95% C.I.	Odds ratio	95% C.I.
Choice				
Did not skip a visit because of cost	2.12***	[1.46; 3.06]	2.34***	[1.97; 2.78]
Co-Production				
Information provided by doctors was easy to understand	2.06**	[1.32; 3.21]	1.70***	[1.43; 2.04]
Patient was involved in health care decisions	1.12	[0.76; 1.67]	1.51***	[1.31; 1.75]
Used patient portals and apps	1.16	[0.90; 1.48]	0.97	[0.87; 1.08]
Integrated Care				
Arrangements and information for follow- up care after hospitalisation	1.49**	[1.14; 1.93]		
Respectful Care				
Doctors and nurses treat patient with respect in hospital	1.97***	[1.37; 2.85]		
Doctor spends enough time with patient	1.55*	[1.09; 2.21]	1.80***	[1.57; 2.06]
Control variables				
Average or above-average income	1.40**	[1.10; 1.79]	1.27***	[1.15; 1.41]
Good health status	1.54**	[1.20; 1.97]	1.45***	[1.27; 1.65]
Female	0.77*	[0.60; 0.98]	0.91	[0.83; 1.01]
Observations	3 289		18 269	
Prob > F	0.000		0.000	

Note: Estimations included a country-level fixed effect to account for the average country-level characteristics of the health system that affect all respondents within a same country. ** Significant at 5% ** Significant at 1% ***Significant at <0.1%.
Source: Authors estimation based on data from The Commonwealth Fund (2020[29]), International Health Policy Survey of Adults, https://www.commonwealthfund.org/series/international-health-policy-surveys.

The results of the regression analysis indicate that people with a more positive experience across the dimensions of choice, co-production, integrated care, and respectful care are significantly more likely to agree that the health system performs well, controlling for income, health status, and gender, and country-level characteristics. Across 11 OECD countries, for the people who were hospitalised in the past 2 years, and when compared with people who did not have the experiences below, the probability of agreeing that the health system performed well was, on average:

- 2.12 times higher for people who did not skip a doctor visit because of cost (choice);

- 2.06 times higher for people who received easy to understand information from the doctors (co-production);

- 1.49 times higher for those who had arrangements made by their hospital for a follow up care after hospitalisation and their usual provider was well-informed about hospitalisation (integration);

- 1.97 times higher for people who reported receiving respectful treatment for doctors and nurses while hospitalised (respectfulness); and

- 1.55 times higher for people who reported that their doctors spent enough time with them (respectfulness).

The results for the larger sample including people who were not hospitalised in the last two years were mostly similar in direction and magnitude of association, and as expected, the precision of the estimates increased. However, no variable was available about integration of care, since the concept of integration necessarily represents different levels or areas of the health system. Across 11 OECD countries, for respondents and when compared with people who did not have the experiences below, the probability of agreeing that the health system performed well was, on average:

- 2.34 times higher for people who did not skip a doctor visit because of cost (choice);
- 1.70 times higher for people who received easy to understand information from the doctors (co-production);
- 1.51 times higher for people who were involved in decisions about their health care (co-production); and
- 1.80 times higher for people who reported that their doctors spent enough time with them (respectfulness).

In both models, people with higher income and with good health status were more likely to agree that their health system performed well. Males were more likely to agree that their health system performed well in the model including people hospitalised in the previous two years only. Age was not included in the model because data was not available for one of the countries, but a sensitivity analysis for the 10 remaining countries including a control variable on age showed very similar results in magnitude, direction, and precision of the estimates.

The analysis confirmed that people who experience their health care system to be people centred are more likely to have confidence in their health system. The more people experienced to have choice in their care, being able to co-produce their care path, experience respect and integrated care, showed to be associated with positive views of the health system and positive self-rated health. The data used in this section derived from The Commonwealth Fund capture data on patient level on a broad range of topics. It covers a geographically diverse sample of OECD countries, including Europe, America and Oceania.

The results in this section confirm the relevance of the dimensions of choice, co-production, respectful care, and integrated care, given their empirical association, at the patient-level, with perception of high performance of the health system. The scorecard was developed to stimulate the discussion of the main domains and policy benchmarks that are relevant for People-Centred Health Systems, to understand how countries might measure domains of people-centredness, and to identify measurement gaps that may impede progress towards strengthening the people-centredness of health systems. It is not intended to rank countries according the levels of people-centredness, nor to provide an aggregated measure.

Improving measurement to strengthen people-centredness

The indicators included in the Scorecard underscore the dearth of relevant, comparable data on key aspects of people-centredness for the health system. There is an urgent need to expand the collection of person-centred indicators beyond the scale up of patient-reported measures. While the focus on scaling up and integrating patient-reported measures is an essential component of assessing health systems performance addresses a critical measurement gap, there has been less attention paid to how to better measure other key components of people-centredness, and how key health systems characteristics – including governance, financing structures, and the overall architecture of health systems delivery – do or do not facilitate the broader delivery of people-centred care. In particular, measures that capture the extent of the embeddedness of the collective patient *voice* – as a complement to the individual-level focus of patient-reported measures – is needed.

At the same time, a key limitation of this benchmarking exercise was that challenges of data comparability and quality precluded the inclusion of certain variables that may have been even more relevant to assessing the people-centredness in certain dimensions. Health literacy, for example, is critically important to informing the ability of individuals to take advantage of the choices available to them within the health system, to make informed decisions as a co-producer of their health, and to self-manage their health

(Moreira, 2018[19]). Yet a lack of comparable cross-country data meant that no measure of health literacy was included in the benchmarking exercise.

A lack of thorough measurement across the five dimensions of people-centred health systems underscores that countries have further to go to delivering systematically people-centred policies, across sectors, services, and levels of the health system. Benchmarking across the five dimensions of the OECD Framework has highlighted that while certain countries appear to perform relatively strongly across the different dimensions of people-centredness, very few countries perform uniformly well across voice, choice, co-production, integration and respectfulness in orienting their health systems to be people centred. Moreover, data availability across all measures and dimensions by country remains inconsistent. The lack of available data to measure progress across all five dimensions underscores how far many countries have to go to better embedding people-centredness as a key actionable principle throughout their health systems. All countries have room to improve the people-centredness of their health systems.

References

Bardon, E. (2021), "An ethical approach to considering family presence during COVID-19", *Healthcare Management Forum*, Vol. 34/3, http://dx.doi.org/10.1177/0840470420980655. [16]

Braun, E. et al. (2009), "Telephone follow-up improves patients satisfaction following hospital discharge", *European Journal of Internal Medicine*, Vol. 20/2, http://dx.doi.org/10.1016/j.ejim.2008.07.021. [25]

Coulter, A. et al. (2015), *Personalised care planning for adults with chronic or long-term health conditions*, http://dx.doi.org/10.1002/14651858.CD010523.pub2. [22]

Davis, K., S. Schoenbaum and A. Audet (2005), "A 2020 vision of patient-centered primary care", *Journal of General Internal Medicine*, Vol. 20/10, pp. 953-957, http://dx.doi.org/10.1111/j.1525-1497.2005.0178.x. [28]

Doty, M. et al. (2021), "Income-related inequality in affordability and access to primary care in eleven high-income countries", *Health Affairs*, Vol. 40/1, pp. 113-120, http://dx.doi.org/10.1377/hlthaff.2020.01566. [27]

Health Foundation. (2016), *Person-centred care made simple : What everyone should know about person-centred care*, Health Foundation, London. [1]

Hoon Chuah, F. et al. (2018), "Community participation in general health initiatives in high and upper-middle income countries: A systematic review exploring the nature of participation, use of theories, contextual drivers and power relations in community participation", *Social Science & Medicine*, Vol. 213, pp. 106-122, http://dx.doi.org/10.1016/j.socscimed.2018.07.019. [8]

Jack, B. et al. (2009), "A reengineered hospital discharge program to decrease rehospitalization", *Annals of Internal Medicine*, Vol. 150/3, http://dx.doi.org/10.7326/0003-4819-150-3-200902030-00007. [26]

Jackson, C. et al. (2015), "Timeliness of outpatient Follow-Up: An Evidence-Based approach for planning after hospital discharge", *Annals of Family Medicine*, Vol. 13/2, http://dx.doi.org/10.1370/afm.1753. [24]

Kelley, E. and J. Hurst (2006), "Health Care Quality Indicators Project: Conceptual Framework Paper", *OECD Health Working Papers*, No. 23, OECD Publishing, Paris, https://dx.doi.org/10.1787/440134737301. [6]

Kruis, A. et al. (2013), "Integrated disease management interventions for patients with chronic obstructive pulmonary disease", *Cochrane Database of Systematic Reviews*, http://dx.doi.org/10.1002/14651858.cd009437.pub2. [23]

Lopes, E., D. Carter and J. Street (2015), "Power relations and contrasting conceptions of evidence in patient-involvement processes used to inform health funding decisions in Australia", *Social Science and Medicine*, Vol. 135, http://dx.doi.org/10.1016/j.socscimed.2015.04.021. [11]

Lopes, E. et al. (2016), "Involving patients in health technology funding decisions: Stakeholder perspectives on processes used in Australia", *Health Expectations*, Vol. 19/2, http://dx.doi.org/10.1111/hex.12356. [12]

Moreira, L. (2018), "Health literacy for people-centred care: Where do OECD countries stand?", *OECD Health Working Papers*, No. 107, OECD Publishing, Paris, https://dx.doi.org/10.1787/d8494d3a-en. [19]

Nolte, E., S. Merkur and A. Anell (2020), *Achieving Person-Centred Health Systems. Evidence, Strategies and Challenges*, Cambridge University Press, Cambridge, UK, http://dx.doi.org/10.1017/9781108855464. [3]

OECD (2021), *Health at a Glance 2021: OECD Indicators*, OECD Publishing, Paris, https://doi.org/10.1787/ae3016b9-en. [21]

OECD (2019), *Health at a Glance 2019: OECD Indicators*, OECD Publishing, Paris, https://doi.org/10.1787/4dd50c09-en. [18]

OECD (2019), *Health for Everyone?: Social Inequalities in Health and Health Systems*, OECD Health Policy Studies, OECD Publishing, Paris, https://dx.doi.org/10.1787/3c8385d0-en. [17]

OECD (2019), *Health in the 21st Century: Putting Data to Work for Stronger Health Systems*, OECD Health Policy Studies, OECD Publishing, Paris, https://dx.doi.org/10.1787/e3b23f8e-en. [20]

OECD (2016), *Health Systems Characteristics Survey*, https://qdd.oecd.org/subject.aspx?Subject=hsc. [13]

OECD Health Care Quality Indicators Expert Group (2015), "Towards actionable international comparisons of health system performance: expert revision of the OECD framework and quality indicators", *International Journal for Quality in Health Care*, http://dx.doi.org/10.1093/intqhc/mzv004. [7]

Rajan, D. et al. (2020), "Governance of the Covid-19 response: a call for more inclusive and transparent decision-making", *BMJ Global Health*, Vol. 5/5, p. e002655, http://dx.doi.org/10.1136/bmjgh-2020-002655. [15]

Richards, T. and H. Scowcroft (2020), "Patient and public involvement in covid-19 policy making", *The BMJ*, Vol. 370, http://dx.doi.org/10.1136/bmj.m2575. [14]

Rozmovits, L. et al. (2018), "What does meaningful look like? A qualitative study of patient engagement at the Pan-Canadian oncology drug review: Perspectives of reviewers and payers", *Journal of Health Services Research and Policy*, Vol. 23/2, http://dx.doi.org/10.1177/1355819617750686. [9]

Santana, M. et al. (2018), *How to practice person-centred care: A conceptual framework*, Blackwell Publishing Ltd, http://dx.doi.org/10.1111/hex.12640. [5]

Santana, M. et al. (2018), "How to practice person-centred care: A conceptual framework", *Health Expectations*, Vol. 21/2, pp. 429-440, http://dx.doi.org/10.1111/hex.12640. [2]

The Commonwealth Fund (2020), *International Health Policy Survey of Adults*, The Commonwealth Fund, https://www.commonwealthfund.org/series/international-health-policy-surveys. [29]

Vanstone, M. et al. (2019), *Ethical Challenges Related to Patient Involvement in Health Technology Assessment*, http://dx.doi.org/10.1017/S0266462319000382. [10]

World Health Organization Regional Office for Europe (2016), *Integrated care models: an overview Working document*, WHO Regional Office for Europe, Copenhagen, https://www.euro.who.int/__data/assets/pdf_file/0005/322475/Integrated-care-models-overview.pdf (accessed on 17 May 2021). [4]

2 Designing policies to deliver people-centred health

This chapter evaluates what OECD countries have done to put in place people-centred policies in their health systems and considers the extent to which countries have promoted people-centredness in their policy making across the dimensions of the OECD Framework for People-Centred Health Systems. It finds that while policies have been adopted that contribute to moving towards a people-centred approach, they are oftentimes inadvertent – though positive – consequences of other policy priorities and goals. There remains a lack of a holistic understanding of how policies across sectors, actors, and levels of governance can build on each other to create a fully people-centred approach.

Results of the benchmarking exercise suggest that countries have not yet maximised putting people at the centre across their health systems. At the same time, growing attention to the importance of person-centredness has meant that there has been an increased focus on taking a people-centred lens to policy making. This chapter reviews the extent to which OECD countries have adopted and implemented policies that support a people-centred approach across the key dimensions of voice, choice, co-production, integration and respectfulness. It draws on the results of the OECD Policy Survey on People-Centred Health Systems to examine what countries have done to move towards a more people-centred approach. Twenty-three countries completed the survey, which was completed before the emergence of SARS-CoV-2 and thus reflects policies in place before the pandemic. Given the extraordinary nature of many of the measures adopted in the context of the COVID-19 pandemic, people's trust and confidence that health systems and governments act in their best interest and with them in mind has only become more relevant.

Voice: Strengthening patient voice in decision-making

Key findings

- While important steps have been taken to strengthen the role of patient voice in health systems decision-making, comparatively fewer countries consider patient voice in systems-level decision-making to be important or very important.

- Fewer than two-thirds of countries (14/22) reported that including patients in decisions about design of benefits packages and funding of health care services was important or very important, compared with more than 90% of countries (21/23) who consider it important or very important to include patients in decisions about their own treatment.

- While there is broad agreement that a people-centred health system is important, there has been more focus on how this can be applied at the micro (patient) level, with less attention to the systemic changes that are required to transform the apparatus of a health system.

Table 2.1. Examples of policies to improve voice in voice in health systems.

Type of policy	Country examples
Decision-making processes for health authorities	**Canada:** The Patient and Family Advisory Council to advise Ontario's Minister of Health and Long-Term Care; Health Standards Organization includes patients and families on its technical committees to provide inputs for health and social service standards.
	Luxembourg: Patients are included on both the boards and working groups responsible for the development of disease-specific national plans.
	Austria, Germany: Patients are included in decision-making processes for insurance funds.
	Australia: The National Safety and Quality Health Service Standards requires health service organisations to partner with consumers through the planning, development, delivery and evaluation of health care services.
Patient safety	**Ireland:** Plans underway to launch strategic co-production groups, including the National Patient Forum and Patients for Patient Safety Ireland.
	Canada: Canadian Patient Safety Institute promotes the participation of patient voice in advancing patient safety; Canadian Foundation of Healthcare Improvement helps to facilitate patient involvement in the design, delivery and evaluation of health services.
	Germany: Opinions and proposals of the national patient safety advocacy group are heard in respective law making processes; integration of patients in working groups on health standards and public information.
Healthcare research or funding for research	**Norway**: Majority of funded projects through both the Research Council of Norway (RCN) and the Regional Health Hospital Authorities (RHA) included public involvement.
	Canada: Canadian Institutes of Health Research's Strategy for Patient-Oriented Research includes patients as active collaborators.

The strong normative argument for involving patients more closely in health care decision-making is clear (Conklin, Morris and Nolte, 2015[1]; Wait and Nolte, 2006[2]). Some have stressed the intrinsic value of including patients in public involvement and decision-making, akin to the democratic process, and have emphasised that beyond the concrete outcomes achieved, involving patients in decision-making can help to influence priority-setting and health policy making over time, and that the benefits can accrue over time (Wait and Nolte, 2006[2]; Thurston et al., 2005[3]).

Beyond the normative argument for including patients in decision-making processes for health, however, there is evidence to suggest that involving patient voices in decision-making can help to improve the relevance and quality of certain aspects of health care. Involving patients and the public in decision-making around research, for example, can help to increase its applicability. In addition to the substantive value they bring through the personal knowledge and expertise from living with their conditions, some have argued that patients have a moral right to involvement, because the decisions taken will affect them, while others have suggested that involving patients helps to improve the success of research (Caron-Flinterman, Broerse and Bunders, 2005[4]; Boote, Telford and Cooper, 2002[5]; Schölvinck, Pittens and Broerse, 2020[6]). Systematic reviews of the impact of patient involvement have found that while further research is needed, involving patients helps to improve the identification of relevant research topics, improves the relevance of the research, better analysed the results from the perspective of both researchers and health systems users, and improved the dissemination and implementation of outcomes (Brett et al., 2014[7]). A review of research studies including patient and public involvement (PPI) in the United Kingdom found that PPI helped contribute to revisions in the design of studies, better recruitment, and improved dissemination of study results (Wilson et al., 2015[8]). Nevertheless, patient involvement in decision-making around research, including priority setting and funding, has been found to lag behind initiatives taken to improve patient voice in health systems (Lloyd and White, 2011[9]; Sacristán et al., 2016[10]).

Including patients in decision-making helps health systems respond better to patient needs

Strengthening patient voice in the development and delivery of health care services can also increase the relevance of available services for users (Bombard et al., 2018[11]). Across a range of health services, involving users in service delivery planning has been found to simplify and improve access to services, including through streamlining appointment processes, prolonging the opening hours of facilities, and better sensitizing services to the needs of people living with disabilities (Crawford et al., 2002[12]). The inclusion of patients in planning processes has been credited with developing new relevant services for patients (Crawford et al., 2002[12]). Staff attitudes towards patients have also been found to improve when service users are involved in health care design (Simpson and House, 2002[13]).

Strengthening patient voice can also help health systems respond better to the need for better co-ordination and integration arising from a shifting burden of disease and demographic change. In a randomised controlled trial of including patients in identifying priorities for health care improvement in Canada, including patients in prioritisation both improved patient-professional agreement on what key priorities and reduced the likelihood that the prioritisation process focused on the management of individual diseases (Boivin et al., 2014[14]).

Patient voice should be better incorporated into governance and systems-level decision-making

Though important steps have been taken in many health systems to strengthen the role of patient voice in health systems decision-making, comparatively fewer countries consider patient voice in systems-level decision-making to be important or very important, when compared with other dimensions of person-centred care. Fewer than two-thirds of countries (14/22) reported that including patients in decisions about design of benefits packages and funding of health care services was important or very important, compared with more than 90% of countries (21/23) who consider it important or very important to include patients in decisions about their own treatment. This gap arguably reflects a key challenge in institutionalising person-centred care: while there is broad agreement that a people-centred health system is important, there has been more focus on how this can be applied at the micro (patient) level, with less attention to the systemic changes that are required to transform the apparatus of a health system.

Sixteen of 23 countries reported that policies are in place or are being discussed to promote the involvement of patients in the organisation, management, and delivery of health care services. Many OECD countries have taken important steps towards increasing the representation of patients in decision-making for health care in recent years. Patient representatives are included in decision-making processes for health authorities in a number of OECD countries, including Austria, Canada, Luxembourg and Germany. In Canada, the government of the province of Ontario has created a Patient and Family Advisory Council to advise the Minister of Health and Long-Term Care in identifying key priorities and issues affecting patient care, while the Health Standards Organization has also included patients and families on its technical committees to provide inputs when the Organization develops or revises health and social service standards. In Luxembourg, patients are included on both the boards and working groups responsible for the development of disease-specific national plans, including for cancer, rare diseases, and cardiovascular diseases. Patients have also been included in the governance of the National Cancer Institute, including in the executive office, on the board of directors, and as part of the scientific advisory board. In Australia, The National Safety and Quality Health Service Standards require health service organisations to partner with consumers in the planning, development, delivery and evaluation of health care services. The Partnering with Consumers Standard also requires health service organisations to partner with consumers in their own care, to the extent they choose.

In some countries, adequate resources have been identified as a barrier to the more systematic inclusion of patient voice. In both Austria and Germany, for example, patients are included in decision-making processes for insurance funds. In Austria, insured populations are primarily indirectly represented, through representatives from employer and worker organisations. Recognising that patient advocacy groups were less systematically included in consultations, social insurance funds, together with the Healthy Austria Fund and the former Ministry of Health and Women, has launched an initiative to strengthen the visibility and activities of patient groups, including to improve patient representation and participation at the federal level. The initiative includes funding to help improve the independence of groups and reduce their dependence on private donations.

Across OECD countries, patient safety is a pressing health concern, with as many as one in ten patients harmed during a hospital admission and as much as 15% of hospital expenditure likely attributable to patient harm (Slawomirski, Auraaen and Klazinga, 2017[15]). Effective patient engagement has been identified as critical in helping to improving patient safety (Slawomirski, Auraaen and Klazinga, 2017[15]). Many OECD countries have taken steps to ensure patients are included in decision-making around patient safety and health service design. In Ireland, for example, plans are currently underway to launch strategic co-production groups, including the National Patient Forum and Patients for Patient Safety Ireland, who will work together with staff from the Health Service Executive on the design and evaluation of health services. In Canada, the Canadian Patient Safety Institute has similarly promoted the participation of patient voice in advancing patient safety, while the Canadian Foundation of Healthcare Improvement has helped to facilitate patient involvement in the design, delivery and evaluation of health services. In Germany the opinions and proposals of the national patient safety advocacy group are heard in respective law making processes and patients are integrated in working groups on health standards and public information. In Austria, the Ministry of Health has established an advisory board for patient safety, in addition to a patient safety association. In Ireland, the Open Disclosure Policy promotes a timely, transparent and compassionate response to promote communication following a patient safety incident.

Fewer countries have taken steps to more systematically include patients in decision-making around health care research or funding for research. An important exception is Norway, where the majority of funded projects through both the Research Council of Norway (RCN) and the Regional Health Hospital Authorities (RHA) – the two major government funding avenues for health care research – included public involvement. All RCN decisions are required to have included public involvement, while the proportion of projects funded through RHA that included public involvement more than tripled between 2014 and 2018, from 20% to 68%. In Canada, the Canadian Institutes of Health Research's Strategy for Patient-Oriented Research includes patients as active collaborators, with patient engagement an integral component of all its programs. Recognising the importance of including patient voice in research, Ireland's Health Service Executive is in the process of setting up a *Patient and Public Involvement in Research Advisory Panel* as part of implementing its 2019-29 Action Plan for Health Research.

Choice: Expanding patient decision-making and improving affordability and access to care

Key findings

- Information about quality is especially important if patient choice is intended to improve access to high-quality care. However, even when information is available, patient decisions are not always necessarily made using quality and outcomes information. Access and affordability continue to constrain choice for many patients.
- Telemedicine can serve as a tool to help to expand patient choice and access to care. The COVID-19 pandemic has accelerated the scale-up of telemedicine in many OECD countries, with 45% of respondents in 22 OECD EU countries reporting that they had used telemedical consultation services during the pandemic.

Table 2.2. Examples of policies to improve choice in health systems

Type of policy	Country examples
Resources to improve access to information on quality	**Austria**: Kliniksuche.at ("clinic search") provides access to information about the quality of health services, through improving public access to quality metrics. **Belgium**: The VIP2 programme in Flanders (Flemish Indicators Project for Patients and Professionals) focuses on defining, developing, and implementing indicators to measure the quality of care. **Israel, Norway**: Online publication of national quality indicators to give patients the opportunity to use important clinical information when making health care-related decisions. **Estonia**: The Estonian Health Insurance Fund calculates and publishes online a selection of clinical care quality indicators for hospitals, as well as indicators related to quality and performance for family physicians. **Costa Rica**: The Costa Rican Social Security Fund publishes a selection of clinical care quality indicators for hospitals, as well as indicators related to quality and performance for physicians. **United States**: Medicare extensively collects quality indicators (including about patient experience, care processes, patient safety and outcomes), turning them into ratings that can be used by patients and caregivers to help inform their choice of health plans and providers.
Resources to facilitate choice in health care providers and facilities	**United States**: The CMS Innovation Center has focused on testing models to expand patient choices, including increasing services and providing additional incentives for providing services in the patient's home or alternative sites of care. **England**: Reforms to promote patient choice and encourage competition.
Resources to facilitate access to services	**Germany**: The Law For Faster Appointments And Better Care expands appointment service points and increases consultation hours to improve access and reduce waiting times.

In recent years, many health systems across the OECD have taken steps to increase the choices of goods and services available to individuals (Costa-Font and Zigante, 2016[16]; Santos, Gravelle and Propper, 2017[17]). These health systems reforms have for many countries been driven by factors beyond – though in many cases including – a normative preference to expand patient's decision-making power in their health systems. Many reforms that have expanded opportunities for patient choice have instead been driven by underlying goals of ensuring the sustainability of health systems by increasing competition and efficiency, particularly where public health systems operate in competition with parallel or supplemental private markets. Some researchers have linked the expansion of choice in health systems to the expectations and demands of the middle class in democratic systems, and have situated such reforms in the broader context of the responsiveness of public policy making more broadly to demands for expanded choice (Blomqvist, 2004[18]; Costa-Font and Zigante, 2016[16]).

Provider choice is widespread in OECD countries

Facilitating choice in health care providers and facilities is seen as an important component of people-centredness. Giving patients a choice in their provider and health facilities is considered to be important or very important in most OECD countries. Most responding countries (20/23) reported that they considered a patient's choice of health care provider, including health care facilities and health care professionals, to be important or very important. In the United States, for example, the CMS Innovation Center has focused on testing models to expand patient choices, including increasing services and providing additional incentives for providing services in the patient's home or alternative sites of care.

In a majority of OECD countries, patients have substantial flexibility in choosing their health care services across multiple levels of the health system, from primary to hospital care. The majority of reporting countries allow patients free choice in choosing their health care provider at the primary care level (18/31 OECD countries), outpatient specialist level (17/31 OECD countries), and hospital level (16/31 OECD countries). Even where free choice is available, roughly a quarter of countries report using financial incentives to guide patient behaviour, particularly at the specialist and hospital level.

Promoting patient choice can help to improve efficiency in some parts of the health system. A number of countries have introduced reforms promoting greater hospital choice for patients with the explicit goals of improving competition. In England, reforms to promote patient choice and encourage competition were found to have led to improvements in hospital efficiency, including on admissions per bed and doctor, as well as the proportion of day cases in hospital (Longo et al., 2019[19]).

Information about quality is especially important if patient choice is intended to improve access to high-quality care. However, even when information is available, patient decisions are not always necessarily made using quality and outcomes information. While countries have increased the availability of quality and outcomes information available to patients, care-seeking behaviours are not always influenced by this information. Evidence from countries that have recently instituted patient choice policies suggests that patients are often influenced by more prosaic factors. In studies of hospital choice, patients in Germany and the Netherlands reported being influenced by factors including the distance from their home to hospital, the recommendation of their general practitioner, the input of family and friends, and online resources (Lako and Rosenau, 2009[20]; De Cruppé and Geraedts, 2017[21]). This may at least in part be attributable to difficulties for patients in readily identifying the information they feel is necessary to make informed choices (Victoor et al., 2016[22]). In a study of choice in primary care in Finland, more than three-quarters of respondents felt choice to be important, but fewer than half felt they had real opportunities to make such choices, with just over one-third of respondents reporting that they were satisfied with the information they received for making choices (Aalto et al., 2018[23]).

Improving access to quality information about the aspects of the *health systems* themselves is important to helping patients make informed decisions about their health and care. Countries have also taken steps to improve the transparency of health systems for patients and users. Eleven of 17 countries reported developing strategies or policies to inform patients about health care quality or costs of providers. Many countries have focused on improving access to information about the quality of health services, through improving public access to quality metrics, such as hospital performance indicators. Portals such as *klin.ksuche* ("clinic search") and *gesundheit.gv.at* in Austria and the VIP2 programme in Flanders (Belgium), as well as the publication online of national quality indicators, as in Israel and Norway, give patients at least the opportunity – whether or not it is taken – to use important clinical information when making health care-related decisions. In Estonia, for example, the Estonian Health Insurance Fund calculates and publishes online a selection of clinical care quality indicators for hospitals, as well as indicators related to quality and performance for family physicians.

Access challenges continue to pose important constraints on exercising choice

Material and geographic constraints can further impact the extent to which patients are able to exercise the choice available to them. More than one in five adults across 23 OECD countries reported postponing or forgoing care due to long waiting times or transportation issues, while one in six reported putting off or forgoing care because of cost (OECD, 2019[24]). Delaying or forgoing care due to access and affordability concerns is particularly common among people of lower socio-economic status: those in the lowest income quintile were 28% more likely to report delaying or forgoing care due to accessibility (waiting time or transportation) issues, and three times more likely to delay or avoid care because of cost (OECD, 2019[24]). In some cases, countries have introduced flexibilities into systems with otherwise limited choice to help overcome these access challenges. In some provincial health systems (Saskatchewan, Ontario) in Canada, for example, when waiting times are too long, patients are given a choice to seek care via a different specialist or hospital with shorter waiting times.

In recent years, there has been a growing interest in the use of telemedicine services – such as telephone and video consultations, and the remote monitoring of chronic conditions – to improve access to care and choice for patients. Patients who have used telemedicine services have reported very high levels of satisfaction with the care they receive, and telemedicine interventions have been found to improve treatment adherence and outcomes, as well as better self-management, for patients with chronic conditions. While patients have been enthusiastic about the possibilities of telemedicine, however, until recently telemedicine services were comparatively infrequent across OECD countries. Evidence from OECD countries suggests that in at least some countries, teleconsultations dramatically increased during the pandemic and were sometimes able to make up for drops in in-person consultations (Figure 2.1).

Figure 2.1. Doctor consultations per capita in 2019 and 2020 by mode of consultation

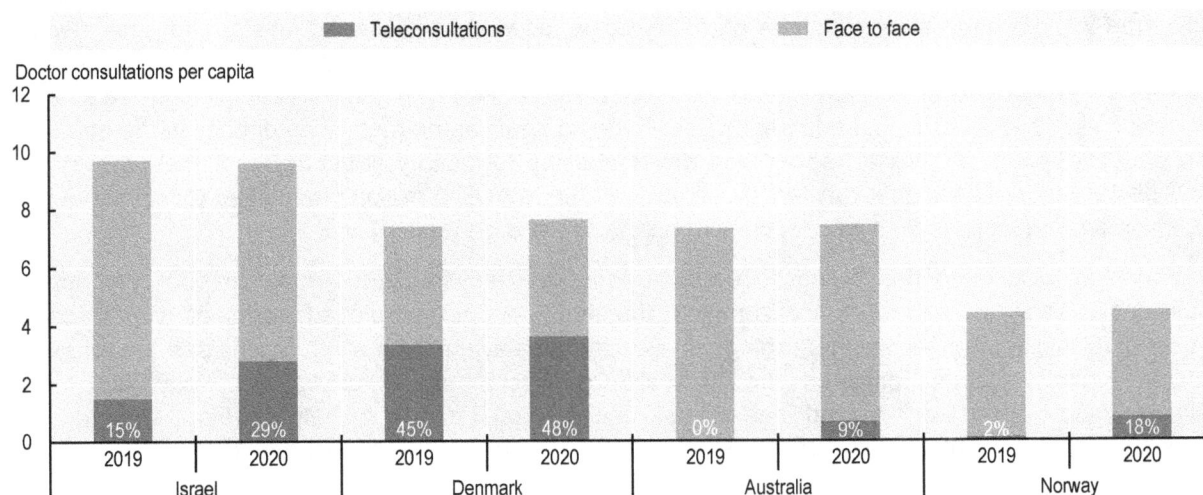

Source: OECD (2021[25]), *Health at a Glance 2021: OECD Indicators*, https://doi.org/10.1787/ae3016b9-en.

In Austria, the national health service line 1450, established before the pandemic, offers telephone consultation and clearing in relation to treatment need seven days a week and 24 hours a day. While the system was not initially planned as an emergency/crisis hotline, it was further developed in the context of COVID-19 to enable residents to be triaged when they suspect a COVID-19 infection. A similar telephone triage service, the SNS24, exists in Portugal and was expanded to adapt to better address the pressures on the health system during the COVID-19 pandemic.

As the uptake of the COVID-19 vaccine has slowed in some countries, creative efforts to reduce access-related barriers have been developed to encourage vaccination and overcome vaccine hesitancy. In Austria, the health system has offered easy-access vaccines through the roll out of mobile vaccination services, which facilitate easier access to vaccination in rural areas and allow individuals to be vaccinated without needing to sign up online.

Box 2.1. How has the COVID-19 pandemic changed how countries use telemedicine?

Telehealth has many potential benefits in the context of COVID-19, both in the treatment of presumed cases of confirmed COVID-19 with mild symptoms, and for ensuring continuity of care, including for people with chronic conditions, in the context of confinement policies. Telehealth – the use of information and communication technologies to promote health at a distance, including non-clinical services and education – has been used in previous disease outbreaks like Ebola and Zika, and supplies a set of tools and applications to prevent spread. While the use of telemedicine in the OECD prior to the pandemic was still low, several countries have relaxed regulatory barriers and started to promote its use at scale in response to COVID-19. In just the first weeks and months of the pandemic, countries and regions that had no telemedicine legislation or reimbursement schedules introduced new services, new fees, new legislation, new guidelines and regulations, and have encouraged its adoption and use. The increase in the adoption and use of telemedicine/telehealth demonstrated the speed with which some barriers – including reimbursement/financing arrangements and provider resistance to virtual care – can be eliminated or mitigated. By February/March 2021, close to half (45%) of respondents in 22 European OECD countries reported that they had undergone a telemedical consultation during the pandemic.

In Australia, the government temporarily added telehealth services to the Medicare Benefits Scheme to mitigate COVID-19 transmission through health care visits. Temporary telehealth benefits were extended to both general practitioners and specialists, as well as nurses, dentists, and other health providers. The Australian Government has also accelerated the delivery of e-prescribing to help vulnerable populations avoid exposure to the virus. Doctors, including general pracitioners, are able to electronically send a prescription to pharmacies, who can deliver the medicines directly to the home of the patient. Though Australia had already developed the regulatory structure for e-prescribing, the COVID-19 pandemic has fast-tracked its roll-out, with up to AUD 5 million channelled to rolling out the technological capacity in 80% of community pharmacies and general practices.

Canada has also expanded billing codes to support telemedicine and virtual care delivery during COVID-19. While telephone care remains the most widely employed form of virtual care, videoconferencing and secure messaging services are also available in all provinces and territories to enable communication between health care providers and patients. In May 2020, the Canadian Government announced investments of CAD 240.5 million to help develop, expand and launch virtual and mental health care tools in the context of the COVID-19 pandemic.

The promotion of telemedicine as a strategy to minimise virus transmission while maintaining access to health services has led to a rapid uptake in the proportion of consultations conducted remotely. In Norway, 37% of primary care consultations in March and April 2020 were teleconsultations, compared with just 2% over the same period in 2019. In Portugal, remote medical consultations in primary health care units grew by 50% in the January-May 2020 period, compared to the previous year. The growth in teleconsultations helped to offset in-person declines in doctor visits in 2020 in Australia, Israel and Norway (OECD, 2021[25]).

Co-production: Promoting patient engagement and empowerment

Key findings

- Patients are increasingly seeking health information to be in greater control of their own health and health care services. Providing curated health information is a way to ensure the quality of advice given to patients. Moreover, improving access to information about health systems gives patients the opportunity to be more engaged in their own care and can improve outcomes and satisfaction. Several countries maintain or support dedicated portals to help patients.

- Enabling people to access their health records and interact with their own medical information is a driver of co-production. While the majority of OECD countries (70%) say they are implementing ways for people to access their health data electronically, fewer than half (43%) include the ability for patients to interact with their own health records, and the data they do have access to is often just a subset of their full health record.

- Health literacy, including digital health literacy, is critical to ensure patients make positive decisions about their health. In 12 of 18 OECD countries with some form of health literacy data, more than half the adult population has low levels of health literacy. However, international comparability of the data is limited.

Table 2.3. Examples of policies to improve co-production in health systems.

Type of policy	Country examples
Provision of curated health-related information	**Austria, United Kingdom:** *Gesundheit.gv.at* in Austria and *NHS Health A-Z* in the United Kingdom compile comprehensive, neutral information related to diseases and health conditions and topics and can serve as a trustworthy resource for individuals going online for information related to their health. **Germany:** Working towards developing government-affiliated websites to provide comprehensive health information to their populations. **Costa Rica:** The Costa Rican Social Security Fund has compiled online information on diseases and health conditions for health systems users to access through the Social Security Fund's website. The Ministry of Health has also developed accessible online platforms that offer tools for patients to learn about their rights and the services offered by the health system.
Resources to help navigate the health system	**Canada:** The Canadian Institute for Health Information maintains the dedicated online platform *Yourhealthsystem.cihi.ca* to inform both the population and policy analysts. **Norway:** *Helsenorge.no* is a guide for citizens wanting to take care of their health, as well as learn about public health care in Norway. Accessible platforms offer tools for patients to learn about their rights and the services offered by the health system. **Israel:** *Kol Briyut* call centre offers information to about the services available under the Health Basket.
Patient's access to their own electronic health records	**Belgium:** has expanded access to electronic records to patients since 2018, allowing patients to access both personal and general health information through the patient portal masante.belgique.be (mijngezondheid.be). **United Kingdom:** Patient Online is an NHS England programme designed to support GP Practices to offer and promote online services to patients, including access to coded information in records, appointment booking and ordering of repeat prescriptions. **Estonia:** Unified EHR enables residents to view all of their medical data in one place – including diagnoses, test results, medications. Residents can also interact with their data. **Lithuania:** A centralised 'one resident – one record' EHR system covers 95% of the population. It carries all relevant medical information in integrated electronic workflows covering appointments, referrals and e-prescribing. It also enables provider interaction and patients have secure access to their record through a patient portal. **Costa Rica:** All citizens have a unique digital health record, which is accessible through an online portal.

Overcoming the traditional health professional-patient model is important to developing a co-productive relationship. This requires developing policies that target both actors. While many policies to improve patient engagement rightly focus on the role of health professionals in better communicating and facilitating a collaborative relationship with their patients, patients also bear ownership over the extent to which they embrace a co-productive approach. In Austria, the adoption of the National Strategy for Improving Healthcare Communication led to a multi-strategic implementation process that includes communication trainings for health professionals and improving the health literacy of health care organisations as well as measures to empower patients in communication (e.g. for asking questions), co-ordinated by the Austrian Health Literacy Alliance. In the context of the COVID-19 pandemic, stakeholder communication measures are being employed, based on an interdisciplinary assessment of needs, to encourage vaccine update and address vaccine hesitancy, particularly among underserved and vulnerable communities. These have included the roll-out of communication strategies targeting individuals whose first language is not German.

Interventions to promote better patient co-production have also been found to improve patient outcomes after hospital procedures (Trummer et al., 2006[26]). In a study of patients undergoing heart surgery in Australia, patients in the intervention group – whose health professionals had undergone additional communications training and who received reorganised patient information services – had shorter lengths of stay in hospital, were released to less intensive care more quickly, and experienced significantly fewer post-surgery complications compared with patients who received traditional care (Trummer et al., 2006[26]). Better communication between patients and health professionals – including more information, and the skills needed to interpret it – have been found to contribute both to higher patient satisfaction and improved patient safety (Slawomirski, Auraaen and Klazinga, 2017[15]). In Austria, an extensive literature review was commissioned on the improvement of communication between professionals and patients, which started the implementation of a National Strategy for Improving Healthcare Communication (adopted 2016).

One major driver of the role of co-production in influencing disease and treatment outcomes is its impact on patient empowerment. Higher levels of patient empowerment have been associated with better disease self-management, including treatment adherence and behavioural change, greater patient literacy, and improved clinical outcomes (Aujoulat, d'Hoore and Deccache, 2007[27]). This is particularly important for health conditions that require active and ongoing patient participation and self-management for good outcomes, including non-communicable disease management and mental health conditions. Shared decision-making that promotes patient participation in making treatment decisions has been found to improve treatment adherence among patients with depression, while shared decision-making has been found to positively influence treatment-related empowerment among patients with psychosis (Loh et al., 2007[28]; Stovell et al., 2016[29]). In an intervention for diabetes patients experiencing disease-related difficulties, a patient-collaboration intervention focused on providing information and facilitating patient empowerment significantly improved clinical outcomes, including blood glucose levels, in addition to improvements in self-rated health and quality of life (Keers et al., 2004[30]).

Digital technologies have expanded the tools of patient co-production – but the quality of information varies, and health literacy levels – including digital health literacy – are not always sufficient

In recent years, the digital transformation of society has led to rapid growth in the number of people using the internet and other digital tools to seek out health information. Between 2008 and 2017, online health-seeking behaviour nearly doubled among adults in 27 OECD countries (OECD, 2019[31]). Patients now have the option to go directly to the source of clinical information, rather than relying on health professionals to interpret it for them.

While access to high-quality sources of information have proliferated, more general concerns about the quality of information available online raise questions about the ability – or in some cases, desire – of individuals to distinguish between established authorities and more dubious health information. While the lack of a 'filter' between individuals and health-related information is positive for patient empowerment, without the sufficient ability to interpret the information presented to them, health outcomes can suffer.

With the proportion of the population seeking out health-related information online, health systems increasingly recognise the importance of ensuring responsible, accurate information is provided to individuals wishing to have a greater understanding of their health and input into decisions around care decisions related to them. Many countries have taken steps to provide access to high-quality information through official websites and health portals, with the explicit aim of providing public-facing quality information, while others have focused on improving health literacy to ensure patients have the proper tools to properly interpret what they find.

In many cases, these resources have been designed specifically to address demands for *health*-related information. Websites such as *gesundheit.gv.at* in Austria and *NHS Health A-Z* in the United Kingdom compile comprehensive, neutral information related to diseases and health conditions and topics and can serve as a trustworthy resource for individuals going online for information related to their health. Recognising the importance of ensuring people are directed towards quality resources when looking for health-related information, other countries, including Germany, are also working towards developing government-affiliated websites to provide comprehensive health information to their populations.

Health systems are complex, and understanding what services, care pathways, or rights patients have can be difficult to navigate even for the most informed. Ensuring patients have access to the tools and resources are available to them is important to facilitating truly co-productive patient engagement. Interactive tools such as *Your Health System* in Canada, the *Kol Briyut* call centre in Israel, which offers information about the services available under the Health Basket, or the *helsenorge* public health website in Norway offer accessible platforms for patients to learn about their rights and the services offered by the health system.

In Australia, health officials have taken steps to increase health literacy around key information related to the COVID-19 pandemic. The broader population has quickly been forced to grasp new, often confusing concepts related to the virus, infection, immunity, and broader access to and use of the health care system and resources. Concepts such as 'flattening the curve' can be poorly understood. To ensure the population is able to best understand the flurry of health information related to the pandemic, authorities have undertaken activities to offer accurate – and localised – information, including developing specific websites, apps, and a dedicated telephone hotline.

Enabling people to access their health records and interact with their own medical information is a driver of high quality people-centred care. Digital technology provides the ideal platform to enable this access easily and efficiently. Belgium has expanded access to electronic records to patients since 2018, allowing patients to access both personal and general health information through the patient portal masante.belgique.be (mijngezondheid.be). Other examples of progress can be found (OECD, 2019[31]). Estonia has a unified EHR, which enables residents to view all of their medical data in one place – including diagnoses, test results, medications. Residents can also interact with their data. For example, they can update their details, supplement existing information, and carry out administrative processes such as obtaining a medical certificate for a driver's license without needing a specific appointment. Lithuania has implemented a centralised 'one resident – one record' EHR system that covers 95% of the population. It carries all relevant medical information in integrated electronic workflows covering appointments, referrals and e-prescribing. It also enables provider interaction and patients have secure access to their record through a patient portal. Australia's My Health Record (MHR) system offers individuals a digital platform that includes records on health status, prescriptions, vaccinations, tests, hospital discharge, advance care planning, and other information. Ninety-nine percent of hospitals and pharmacies, and 97% of hospitals, are registered to use the system, which now includes more than 23 million individual MHR (Australian Digital Health Agency, 2021[32]).

Adequate health literacy is essential for individuals to access, process and apply information relevant to their health and make decisions or adapt behaviours accordingly. Individuals with higher levels of health literacy have been found to have higher levels of self-management and self-care, contributing to better clinical outcomes for chronic conditions (Moreira, 2018[33]). Higher health literacy is also associated with enhanced health information-seeking behaviour. Individuals with higher health literacy have been found to be more likely to access and actively use patient portals, compared with individuals with lower levels of health literacy (OECD, 2019[31]). Poor health literacy has been associated with poorer overall health for older adults, including poorer medications adherence and a higher risk of mortality (Moreira, 2018[33]). Misinterpreting health information due to poor health literacy, for example, can contribute to harmful health behaviours, including poor medications adherence or support for unproven or debunked medical claims, such as vaccine hesitancy (Khan and Socha-Dietrich, 2018[34]; Moreira, 2018[33]).

The majority of OECD countries reported that involving patients in decisions about their own care, and ensuring patients are treated respectfully and compassionately by the health system, are important or very important aspects of a people-centred health system. Ensuring patients have adequate health literacy to participate in decisions around their health and care is critical. Yet despite efforts across OECD countries to improve overall health literacy, a high proportion of the adult population in many countries continues to have difficulty accessing and interpreting health information. In 12 of 18 OECD countries with data, more than half the adult population demonstrated low levels of health literacy (Moreira, 2018[33]). At least one-third of adults demonstrate low health literacy across most OECD countries (Moreira, 2018[33]). Despite the interest in the topic of health literacy, progress towards its measurement at the system-level is still uneven across countries and availability of internationally comparable health literacy data is very limited.

Skill gaps among health care workers can impede a co-productive relationship with patients

Health systems increasingly recognise the need to equip health care professionals with the skills needed to meet the changing – and increasingly complex – needs of the population. Countries have increasingly recognised the importance of fostering transversal skills, including better communication, analytical skills, and openness, and have worked to identify and rectify clear skills gaps among health care workers (OECD, 2018[35]). Policymakers have identified the mismatch between the skills health care professionals have, and those they need, as one of the most pressing concerns for health systems today (OECD, 2016[36]).

One approach to rectify this challenge has been to develop skills assessment instruments that work to identify skill needs and gaps among health care professionals and develop strategies to bridge these gaps. While many of these tools have identified skills that reflect clearly the needs of a more person-centred health system – including ensuring health professionals are equipped not only with clinical skills, but the social and communication skills to ensure patients are engaged and treated respectfully – few assessment instruments have been designed specifically with a person-centred approach in mind. This is to a large extent due to the fact that assessment tools have been developed by health care providers, often without input from patients and health systems users themselves (OECD, 2018[35]).

Respectfulness: Ensuring people are valued in the health system

Key findings

- Across a subset of OECD countries, nearly nine in ten patients reported that they received easy-to-understand explanations related to their health, and more than four-fifths of surveyed patients reported that their doctor spent enough time at them during their consultation.

- Nearly all OECD countries (27/31) report that they have a formal definition of patient rights at the national level, and most countries have established ombudsmen who can help to mediate disagreements.

- Patient-oriented general skills of health professionals are necessary to deliver person-centred care. Policies to promote co-production from the health professional perspective are needed to improve communication skills and attitude towards a more active role for patients, but few countries report using them.

- Eleven of 18 OECD countries reported collecting some form of measures of patient experience and outcomes, but their use is far from being systemic in most countries, and international comparability of the measures is limited.

- The Patient-Reported International Survey (PaRIS) of patients with chronic conditions will allow for cross-country comparisons about people's experiences of care and how they assess the results of the services provided by their health systems. This will help policy makers identify best practices, fuel international learning, and foster a dialogue with patients and service providers about how to further improve the performance and people-centredness of health systems.

Table 2.4. Examples of policies to improve respectfulness in health systems.

Type of policy	Country examples
Official channel to report mistreatment or rights violations or Aggregation of data on patient complaints	**Austria:** Hospitals are mandated to report number of patient complaints and how they were handled. **Canada**, the Czech Republic, Germany, Ireland, Norway, Turkey, United States: Ombudsmen who can help to mediate disagreements, either between health care institutions (such as hospitals) and patients, or across the health system more broadly at the national level. Ireland: Complaints Management System (CMS) standardises data for complaints throughout the organisation. **Costa Rica**: A complaints management system run through the Comptroller of Services of the Social Security Fund helps to mediate disagreements between health care institutions and patients, as well as across the health system more broadly.
Skills for health professionals	**Austria, Mexico**: National guidelines and strategies to improve the quality of communication by health care professionals, including to better address the needs of minority populations. **Belgium**: Patient Participation Culture Tool has been developed for health care workers to measure what factors from the health care professional's side impact patient participation and engagement, as well as information sharing. **Japan**: A "concierge" integrated care programme has promoted the participation of the patient as a member of their own care team.
Institutionalising patient-reported experience measures	**Belgium**: Patient-reported experience measures are collected at the hospital level, and have been included as an indicator in their Pay for Performance programme since 2018. Hospitals in Flanders are required to measure and public indicators of quality of care, including PREMs. **Canada**: Acute care patient-reported experience measures are regularly collected through the Canadian Institute for Health Information. **Israel:** Ministry of Health regularly undertakes PREMS with the explicit purpose of receiving feedback on the patient-centredness of health care professionals **Japan**: The Ministry of Health, Labour and Welfare regularly surveys people who sought hospital services, both as inpatients or outpatients. **Lithuania:** Collecting and reporting patient-reported measures are an accreditation requirement for personal health care institutions. Law on Healthcare Institutions includes patient satisfaction

Type of policy	Country examples
	Mexico: Patient satisfaction reporting in the Encuesta de Satisfacción, Trato Adecuado y Digno
	Norway: The Norwegian Institute of Public Health (NIPH) plans to include yearly PREMS for adult hospital patients between 2019-24.
	Spain: Patient-reported measures in the annual Health Barometer population survey.
	Sweden: Patient experiences measures from contact with the health system are included in an annual nation-wide assessment of patient experience.
	United Kingdom (Wales): Patient-reported health and social care experience measures are used to track performance.
	United States: Centers for Medicare and Medicaid (CMS) regularly survey a random percentage of beneficiaries to monitor patient experiences.

Positive relationships with health care providers are important both for patient experience and outcomes of care

In recent years, health systems have put a growing focus on strengthening communication between health care professionals – and in particular, physicians – and their patients. Patients who feel empathy from their physicians report greater satisfaction with their care and have been found to be more likely to comply with medical regimes than patients who experienced a lack of empathy (Kim, Kaplowitz and Johnston, 2004[37]). Higher satisfaction in a physician-patient relationship, including greater trust, has been associated with better clinical outcomes, including among patients with lower back pain, as well as with greater patient satisfaction and lower emotional distress for patients with cancer (Farin, Gramm and Schmidt, 2013[38]; Zachariae et al., 2003[39]).

The impact of a negative relationship between health care providers and patients has also been found to negatively affect health outcomes and quality of care. In particular, the effects of perceived discrimination by physicians on the outcomes of patients has been extensively documented, and found to be associated with an delaying or forgoing necessary medical care, including mental health services (Burgess et al., 2008[40]; Lee, Ayers and Jacobs Kronenfeld, 2009[41]). Among diabetes patients who had experienced perceived racial or ethnic discrimination, the probability of receiving key preventive tests, including a foot exam, blood pressure exam, or haemoglobin A1C test, was 50% lower than those who had not experienced perceived racial discrimination (Ryan, Gee and Griffith, 2008[42]).

Patient-reported data from across OECD countries suggests that, overall, patients broadly report satisfaction with their care. Across a subset of OECD countries, nearly nine in ten reporting that they received easy-to-understand explanations related to their health, and more than four-fifths of surveyed patients reported that their doctor spent enough time at them during their consultation.

Patient rights and recourse for maltreatment are well defined most countries

An official channel to report mistreatment or rights violations can serve as an important measure of accountability for patients vis-à-vis the health system. Nearly all OECD countries (27/31) report that they have a formal definition of patient rights at the national level. Reporting mechanisms that offer patients the opportunity to complain about their treatment are commonplace in OECD countries. Most countries – including Canada, the Czech Republic, Germany, Ireland, Norway, Poland, Turkey and the United States – have established ombudsmen who can help to mediate disagreements, either between health care institutions (such as hospitals) and patients, or across the health system more broadly at the national level. While such recourse is important, these channels arguably function as measures of last resort. Many less extreme experiences with the health system, even where unpleasant or where a patient felt they were not treated with respect, will not rise to the level that a patient would feel the need to resort to official channels of complaint. Yet they can nonetheless have a deleterious impact on the patient's experience with the health system, or impact the care that they receive. Ensuring patients have sufficient recourse to address difficulties with the health system is critical to providing an institutionalised measure of responsibility, even where behaviour is not so egregious as to warrant official complaint.

Aggregated data on patient complaints gathered through such channels can serve as an important tool for measuring how a health system is or is not meeting the needs of its patients. In Ireland, for example, a Complaints Management System (CMS) was developed in response to recommendations by the Health Service Executive Ombudsman's report, which called for the development of a standardised database for the capture and collation of complaints throughout the organisation in order to manage complaints and identify emerging trends. In Austria, for example, hospitals are mandated to report quality measures including the number of patient complaints and how they were handled. In Poland, the Patients' Rights Ombudsman annually presents a report on patient rights in Poland to the Council of Ministers and lower house of the Polish Parliament.

Table 2.5. Countries with formal definition for patient rights and institutions responsible for patient right violations

Country	Formal definition of patients' rights at the national level?	Institution(s) responsible for handling reported violations against the patients charter
Australia	Yes	Each state and territory has a mechanism (Commission for Health Complaints) for reporting health complaints.
Austria	Yes	courts and administrative authorities
Belgium	Yes	Inspection services at subnational levels
Canada	No	
Switzerland	No	
Chile	Yes	Superintendent of Health
Costa Rica	Yes	The national legislation states that all health services (public and private) must have a "Services Comptroller" which must give assistance and investigate any complaint of patients.
Czech Republic	Yes	Ministry of Health and Public Defender of Rights
Germany	Yes	Patients can report violations to the "Patientenbeauftragten"
Denmark	Yes	Danish Patient Safety Authority
Spain	Yes	National level: Ombudsman who manage the claims and suggestions regarding rights and obligations, included user of health system.
Estonia	No	
Finland	Yes	National Supervisory Authority for Welfare and Health, Regional State Administrative Agencies
France	Yes	
United Kingdom	Yes	Parliamentary and Health Service Ombudsman, Local Government Ombudsman, or the Courts
Greece	Yes	
Ireland	Yes	Health Service Executive; Office of the Ombudsman; Ombudsman for Children.
Iceland	Yes	The Ministry of Welfare; The Directorate of Health; The Ministry of Justice.
Israel	Yes	The Ministry of Health
Italy	Yes	Local Health Agencies
Japan	Yes	
Lithuania	Yes	State Healthcare Accreditation Agency under the Ministry of Health, The Commission on Evaluation of Damage Inflicted upon the Health of Patients under the Ministry of Health
Luxembourg	Yes	Ombudsman for children, Ombudsman for the health care sector
Latvia	Yes	Health Inspectorate of Latvia
Mexico	Yes	National Arbitration Medical Commission of the Ministry of Health.
Netherlands	Yes	Inspectorate
Norway	Yes	Fylkesmannen
Poland	Yes	Patients' Rights Ombudsman, Minister of Health, National Health Fund.
Portugal	Yes	Health Regulation Authority (Entidade Reguladora da Sade ERS)
Slovenia	Yes	Representatives of patients' rights, National Commission for Protection of patients' rights
Sweden	No	
Turkey	Yes	Patient Rights Boards
South Africa	Yes	Health Professions Council of South Africa (HPCSA)

Source: OECD (2016[43]), Health Systems Characteristics Survey.

OECD countries are increasingly recognising the importance of developing cross-cutting, transversal skills that can help health professionals to institutionalise compassionate and respectful relationships with patients. Some countries, such as Austria and Mexico, have developed national guidelines and strategies to improve the quality of communication by health care professionals, including to better address the needs of minority populations. Health care professional-facing tools can also help to encourage health care workers to consider how their behaviour impacts the patient-practitioner relationship. In Belgium, the *Patient Participation Culture Tool* has been developed for health care workers to measure what factors from the health care professional's side impact patient participation and engagement, as well as information sharing.

Few countries have taken steps from the health care provider perspective to include patients as co-productive members of their own health care teams. This requires an approach that both encourages patients to engage more actively in their own care, and that works to overcome the resistance among many health care professionals to engage with patients co-productively (Palumbo, 2016[44]). In Japan, a "concierge" integrated care programme has promoted the participation of the patient as a member of their own care team, which has led to an improvement in the behaviour and attitudes of the health professionals involved in the programme (Taneda, 2016[45]; OECD, 2018[35]).

Countries have scaled up patient-reported measures, but collection is not always systematic

Over the last decade, OECD countries have markedly scaled up their use of patient-reported measures to inform health care policy making (Fujisawa and Klazinga, 2017[46]). A number of countries have reported collecting measures of patient-reported experience measures (PREMs) or patient-reported outcome measures (PROMs) and developing channels of patient input to inform the performance and person-centredness of their health systems. Eleven of 18 OECD countries reported collecting measures of PREMs, which measure how patients experience health care and refers to practical aspects of care, such as accessibility, care co-ordination and provider-patient communication. A few countries also reported collection of data on PROMs. These indicators are an important component of ensuring the people-centredness of the health system as a whole. However, collection of PREMs and PROMs is far from being systematic in most countries, and international comparability of these measures is limited.

In Belgium, patient-reported experience measures are collected at the hospital level, and have been included as an indicator in their Pay for Performance programme since 2018. Hospitals in Flanders are required to measure and public indicators of quality of care, including PREMS, and plans are underway to develop reporting mechanisms at the federal level. Adult hospital patients also regularly report patient experiences in Norway, where the Norwegian Institute of Public Health (NIPH) plans to include yearly PREMS for adult hospital patients between 2019-24. Continuous monitoring is also planned for adult mental health patients, as well as patients who receive treatment for substance dependence. Collecting and reporting patient-reported measures are an accreditation requirement for personal health care institutions in Lithuania. The Israeli Ministry of Health regularly undertakes PREMS with the explicit purpose of receiving feedback on the patient-centredness of health care professionals, while in Japan, the Ministry of Health, Labour and Welfare regularly surveys people who sought hospital services, both as inpatients or outpatients. In the United States, the Centers for Medicare and Medicaid (CMS) regularly survey a random percentage of beneficiaries to monitor patient experiences. Also in the United States, the Consumer Assessment of Health Providers and Systems surveys, which measure patient and caregiver experiences with care, are included as part of the evaluation for all model tests run under the CMS Innovation Center.

The inclusion of patient-reported measures annual *Health Barometer* population survey in Spain, and patient satisfaction reporting in the *Encuesta de Satisfacción, Trato Adecuado y Digno (ESTAD)* in Mexico further examples of collection and reporting of some form of national PREMs. In Lithuania, the Law on

Healthcare Institutions was revised in 2018 to explicitly include patient satisfaction – including the number of complaints received annually and the proportion of complaints found to be valid. Alongside this legal revision, the government is in the process of implementing a quality monitoring system for health care institutions that includes patient-reported measures. In the United Kingdom (Wales), patient-reported health and social care experience measures are included to track progress, including the proportion of people who rate their care and support as good or excellent, as well as those who feel included and involved in decisions about their care and support.

In Canada, acute care patient-reported outcome measures are regularly collected through the Canadian Institute for Health Information and Cancer Care Ontario regularly collects patient-reported outcome measures for cancer, while in Sweden, patient experiences measures from contact with the health system are included in an annual nation-wide assessment of patient experience. While some of these measures align with the OECD Patient-Reported Indicators Survey (PaRIS), an important knowledge gap persists about the results of primary and ambulatory care in OECD countries in an international perspective. The *PaRIS* International Survey of People Living with *Chronic Conditions* will be a key tool to increase people-centredness of health systems in OECD countries.

Box 2.2. The Patient Reported Indicator Surveys (PaRIS).

The Patient Reported Indicator Surveys (PaRIS) support the creation and collection of state-of-the-art, internationally comparable patient-reported indicators to advance high performing, people-centred health systems. The PaRIS survey, currently under development, will be the first international survey of patient-reported health outcomes and experiences of people living with one or more chronic conditions who are treated in primary or ambulatory care.

Findings from the survey will fill an important knowledge gap about the results of primary and ambulatory care in OECD countries. It will allow for cross-country comparisons about people's experiences of care and how they assess the results of the services provided by their health systems. This will help policy makers identify best practices, fuel international learning, and foster a dialogue with patients and service providers about how to further improve the performance and people-centredness of health systems and primary care services. Developing the PaRIS survey on an international level will offer an unprecedented opportunity to benchmark the results of health systems and to promote international collaboration to greatly increase the evidence base on effective strategies to support people-centred care.

PaRIS will also collect information on other key aspects of people centredness, including Patient-Reported Outcome Measures (PROMs), which provide information on how patients assess the results of the care they receive, and integration and continuity of care.

Integration: Strengthening the role of primary care and digital tools to improve co-ordination of care

Key findings

- Thirteen out of eighteen responding countries reported that concrete policies to promote care co-ordination within the health system have been implemented, with five indicating that they are under discussion, including financing for integration or reporting integration-related indicators. Seven countries reported developing performance metrics that monitor progress towards better care integration and co-ordination.

- In many cases, integration measures have been developed for specific care pathways or diseases. However, countries are increasingly focusing on the role of primary health care in care co-ordination strategies, which is becoming a focal point for integration strategies.

- Strengthening primary care and multi-disciplinary teams could contribute to better co-ordination and integration across the health system. Nearly all countries have developed or are developing multi-disciplinary teams of health professionals to deliver more co-ordinated care to patients, and many of these are focused on the primary care level.

- Countries have put a major focus on the potential of digital tools to help solve integration challenges. The use of electronic health records has received substantial attention for its potential to improve integration across the health system. While there has been progress towards the uptake of electronic records, establishing linkages and integration between the use of electronic records has been slower. Primary care settings, in particular, have often been excluded from closer integration with other electronic health systems.

- Ten out of 19 responding countries reported implementing policies to strengthen co-ordination between the health and social care sectors, with most others reported that such policies are at least under discussion or have been announced (8/19).

Table 2.6. Examples of policies to improve integration in health systems.

Type of policy	Country examples
Incentives, financing, and tools for care co-ordination	**Belgium, the Czech Republic, Sweden**: performance metrics that monitor progress towards better care integration and co-ordination, for specific care pathways or diseases
	Czech Republic: General Health Insurance Fund (VZP) launched new service codes and reimbursement mechanisms to better incentivise the development and use of patient pathways between oncological treatment centres and other health care providers to improve care integration for patients with cancer.
	Estonia: Care pathway pilot studies are underway in for stroke and cancer, with the goal to create a financing system that incentivise a co-ordinated, person-centred treatment pathway.
	Estonia: Quality bonus system to incentivise the performance of family doctors in chronic disease management, among other areas.
	Israel: Ministry of Health has taken steps to publicise the results of the Quality Indicators Report, which includes measures monitoring integration and co-ordination of care.
	Norway: Piloting primary health care teams that transition away from predominantly fee-for-service payments, towards payment methods for care over time or for bundled services, as well as towards targeted funding from local authorities for hiring additional categories of professionals into physician-owned practices or primary health care physician co-operatives.
	United States: Many Innovation Center models for primary care and episode-based payments incentivise co-ordinated or integrated care among providers.

Type of policy	Country examples
Use of care co-ordinators	**Lithuania**: Primary care institutions with at least 10 000 patients are required to employ a care co-ordinator, who is responsible for co-ordinating preventive screening and health services for patients living with chronic conditions. **Norway:** strengthen the links between primary care and specialist health services through appointing care co-ordinators to strengthen pathways of care. Sweden: Primary care clinics in are required to assign a care co-ordinator to a patient needing health or social care support following a hospital stay.
Promotion of multidisciplinary teams and task-shifting	**Austria**: multi-disciplinary teams are a requirement for innovative primary health care units where core teams of two to three general practitioners are complemented by nurses, administrative staff, and other health professionals, including paediatricians, therapists, or in some cases social workers. **Belgium**: Multi-disciplinary team meetings (multidisciplinaire oncologische consult, MOC) have been introduced in to improve care management for people with cancer to strengthen continuity of care and ensure patients receive more timely diagnosis and treatment. **Canada:** Primary Care Networks comprised of doctors, nurse practitioners, pharmacists, and community care centres offer access to co-ordinated health services in British Columbia, while in Manitoba, teams of providers including physicians, nurses, midwives, and community workers provide co-ordinated team-based care under the Service Co-ordination Framework for Primary Care. Use of multi-disciplinary health teams to promote integrated, community-based care has also been encouraged in the province of Ontario through the use of bundled payments. **Costa Rica**: Multi-disciplinary teams are a requirement for innovative primary care units, where core teams of a general practitioner are complemented by a nurse, administrative staff, and other health professionals. Primary Care Networks comprised of doctors, nurse practitioners, pharmacists and community care centres also offer access to co-ordinated health services. Multi-disciplinary teams are also required in palliative health care units and long-term care, including for at-home long-term and palliative care. **Germany**: The Federal Ministry of Health has launched a strategy process to promote multi-disciplinary teams, with the goal of strengthening the role of nurses and identifying the tasks and responsibilities nurses can take on in addition to their current competencies. **Japan**: Ministry has promoted task-shifting as an avenue to help reform the work style of medical doctors. **Lithuania**: Multi-disciplinary teams are active in general practice, outpatient dental care, and primary mental health services
Use of e-health solutions and digital tools for integration	**Austria, Belgium, Canada, Israel, Lithuania, Luxembourg, and the United Kingdom (Wales):** reported using e-health solutions and digital tools to improve integration and co-ordination within health systems. **Austria**: the electronic health records system Elektronische Gesundheitskarte (ELGA) was launched in hospitals in 2015, and expanded to pharmacies and physicians in private practice in 2018. **Belgium**: Financial incentives to encourage the scale-up of e-health services, including electronic prescribing. The Belgian health system performance report also includes performance metrics focused on the take-up of electronic health services as part of measuring progress towards better care integration and co-ordination, including the proportion of patients with a global medical record registered with a general practitioner. **Canada** has also focused on scaling up the use of electronic prescribing and other e-health initiatives and recently committed CAD 300 million over five years to expand e-prescribing, increase EHR use and improve linkages between EHR systems, and improve patient access to health records. **Estonia**: the government is harnessing its advanced digital capacity to improve the interoperability of registries and administrative datasets for individuals with needs for integrated care and vocational support.
Integration of health care, long-term care and social services	**Japan**: Since 2018, co-ordination at the municipal level between home medical care and long-term care so that older people who require support from both medical and long-term care can continue to live at home until the end of their lives. **Norway**: Anybody requiring long-term health and social care services is entitled to an individual care plan, if they would like one.

People and health systems continue to bear the costs of poor integration

As demographic change transforms the burden of disease across OECD countries, people will increasingly need support from across different levels of the health care system, as well as assistance from both health- and social care. This is particularly true for people living with chronic conditions, as well as those who will ultimately require long-term care support. Better integrating health care – as well as better integrating health and social care – can facilitate health promotion, and poor integration has regularly been identified as key barrier to delivering better person-centred, community-based care.

Evidence from across OECD countries suggests the cost of poor integration and co-ordination is high. In the hospital sector, for example, delayed discharges and hospital readmissions contribute significantly to overall health spending. Caring for a patient in an acute hospital for whom care in other settings is appropriate is expensive. Hospital spending accounts for a significant proportion of overall health spending in OECD countries, with overall hospital spending comprising 38% of health spending in OECD countries (OECD, 2019[24]).

Estimates further suggest that delayed discharges and hospital readmissions contribute substantially to hospital costs. Studies have indicated that the additional bed days occupied by patients ready to be discharged from hospital could comprise between 11% and 31% of overall hospital costs (Landeiro, Leal and Gray, 2016[47]). The costs of delayed discharge stem both from the additional days in hospital accrued by patients otherwise ready to leave, as well as the follow-on effect these additional days have on other hospital services. Occupied beds cannot be used for other patients who may require inpatient acute care, creating bed shortages and delaying transfers of care within hospitals, such as from the emergency ward. A cross-country systematic review of economic studies of delayed discharge estimated that the cost of delayed discharges averages between about GBP 200-565 (EUR 230-650) per patient per day (Rojas-García et al., 2017[48]). While not all hospital readmissions are preventable, many are likely avoidable with better and more co-ordinated care in the community. In a study of a telephone intervention administered to patients following hospital discharge, for example, people who received a post-discharge follow-up call were 23% less likely to be readmitted to hospital within 30 days

Poor co-ordination between hospitals and community-based services has been recognised as a key contributor to delayed discharges and hospital readmissions for more than 30 years (Barker et al., 1985[49]; Shepperd et al., 2013[50]). Even with advancements in digital communication services, hospitals continue to implement discharge planning processes which are poorly co-ordinated with external services. In many cases, discharge planning begins at the end of a hospital stay, limiting the time that hospitals, patients and communities have to prepare for post-discharge support. Co-ordination remains fragmented in too many cases. In response, some countries have taken steps to change the governance of health and social care, in some cases merging all or parts of the two systems. In other cases, steps toward integration occur at a much more micro level, focusing on improving interdisciplinary responses.

All responding countries reported that that concrete policies to promote better care co-ordination within the health system have either been implemented (13/18) or are under discussion or were recently announced (5/18). Many countries (including Austria, Belgium, Canada, Israel, Lithuania, Luxembourg, and the United Kingdom – Wales) reported using e-health solutions and digital tools to improve integration and co-ordination within health systems. Other countries report working to strengthen primary care services and general practice (Austria, Japan, Lithuania), or to strengthen the links between primary care and specialist health services through appointing care co-ordinators to strengthen pathways of care (Lithuania, Norway). More than half of responding countries (10/19) also reported implementing policies to strengthen co-ordination between the health and social care sectors, with most others reporting that such policies are at least under discussion or have been announced (8/19).

Seven countries reported developing performance metrics that monitor progress towards better care integration and co-ordination. In many cases, these measures have been developed for specific care pathways or diseases, such as cancer (Belgium, the Czech Republic, Sweden). In Sweden, for example, standardised pathways for investigating and diagnosing cancer include time frames for significant steps along the pathway, as well as assessment measures for patient flow. Based on this cancer care pathway, Sweden has now begun a national project to develop standardised pathways of care across other diseases. In Israel, the Ministry of Health has taken steps to publicise the results of the Quality Indicators Report, which includes measures monitoring integration and co-ordination of care. In presenting the results of the exercise on a public-oriented online platform, health care providers are encouraged to incentivise – through public pressure – to improve their outcomes. In the Czech Republic, the General Health Insurance Fund (VZP) launched new service codes and reimbursement mechanisms to better incentivise the development and use of patient pathways between oncological treatment centres and other health care providers to improve care integration for patients with cancer. Care pathway pilot studies are underway in

Estonia for stroke and cancer, with the goal to create a financing system that incentivise a co-ordinated, person-centred treatment pathways for the conditions.

Countries are increasingly focusing on the role of primary care in care co-ordination strategies. In Estonia, for example, a quality bonus system has been developed to incentivise the performance of family doctors in chronic disease management, among other areas. To promote person-centred care co-ordination for people with complex needs, focused on the primary care level, a care co-ordinator role has been established to connect patients between their primary health care provider and other services offered in the social care system. Primary care clinics in Sweden are required to assign a care co-ordinator to a patient needing health or social care support following a hospital stay. Where the attending physician in hospital determines a patient requires a care plan following hospitalisation, the primary care clinic is also responsible for the plan. In Lithuania, primary care institutions with at least 10 000 patients are required to employ a care co-ordinator, who is responsible for co-ordinating preventive screening and health services for patients living with chronic conditions.

Nearly all countries have developed or are developing multi-disciplinary teams of health professionals to deliver more co-ordinated care to patients. Many of these are focused on the primary care level. In primary care, team- or network-based primary care models have been found to better serve the needs of a people-centred system by offering more services (often closer to home), while also delivering lower costs and economies of scale to the health system overall (OECD, 2020[51]). People-centred primary care models have been developed or are in the process of being set up in at least 15 OECD countries (OECD, 2020[51]).

Primary Care Networks comprised of doctors, nurse practitioners, pharmacists, and community care centres offer access to co-ordinated health services in British Columbia, Canada, while in Manitoba, teams of providers including physicians, nurses, midwives, and community workers provide co-ordinated team-based care under the Service Co-ordination Framework for Primary Care. These multi-disciplinary teams work together both in-person and virtually, depending on the needs of the local community. The use of multi-disciplinary health teams to promote integrated, community-based care has also been encouraged in the province of Ontario through the use of bundled payments. Norway is currently piloting primary health care teams, with the pilot transitioning away from predominantly fee-for-service payments, towards payment methods for care over time or for bundled services, as well as towards targeted funding from local authorities for hiring additional categories of professionals into physician-owned practices or primary health care physician co-operatives.

In Japan, the ministry has promoted task-shifting as an avenue to help reform the work style of medical doctors. Other countries have promoted a multi-disciplinary team approach in primary care. In Lithuania, for example, multi-disciplinary teams are active in general practice, outpatient dental care, and primary mental health services, while multi-disciplinary teams are a requirement for innovative primary health care units in Austria, where core teams of two to three general practitioners are complemented by nurses, administrative staff, and other health professionals, including paediatricians, therapists, or in some cases social workers. Multi-disciplinary team meetings (*multidisciplinaire oncologische consult, MOC*) have also been introduced in Belgium to improve care management for people with cancer to strengthen continuity of care and ensure patients receive more timely diagnosis and treatment. In Germany, the Federal Ministry of Health has launched a strategy process to promote multi-disciplinary teams, with the goal of strengthening the role of nurses and identifying the tasks and responsibilities nurses can take on in addition to their current competencies.

Health systems have increasingly turned to digital tools to strengthen co-ordination of care

Countries have put a major focus on the potential of digital tools to help solve co-ordination challenges in health care systems. In particular, the use of electronic health or medical records (EHR or EMR) has received substantial attention for its potential to improve integration across disparate parts of the health system. In recent years, OECD countries have made significant progress in moving towards the use of electronic records. While there has been substantial progress made towards the uptake of electronic records, however, establishing linkages and integration between the use of electronic records has been slower, with just 64% of OECD countries reporting that data can be exchanged across a secure integrated network (Oderkirk, 2017[52]; OECD, 2019[31]). Primary care settings, in particular, have often been excluded from closer integration with other electronic health systems. This can mean that information recorded in primary care may not be transmitted to other patient settings, such as hospitals, or that information from a hospital visit is not necessarily shared with a patient's primary care provider, hampering effective, patient-centred co-ordination of care.

Many countries report policies to strengthen the use of electronic records in primary care are underway. In Austria, the electronic health records system *Elektronische Gesundheitskarte* (ELGA) was launched in hospitals in 2015, and expanded to pharmacies and physicians in private practice in 2018. Plans are underway to further expand the use of ELGA in laboratories and radiology, allowing ELGA to ultimately serve as the infrastructure for patient-facing eHealth applications, including electronic vaccination passports. In Belgium, the government has introduced financial incentives to encourage the scale-up of ehealth services, including electronic prescribing. A quarter of physicians and 37% of dentists currently issue electronic prescriptions. The Belgian health system performance report also includes performance metrics focused on the take-up of electronic health services as part of measuring progress towards better care integration and co-ordination, including the proportion of patients with a global medical record registered with a general practitioner. Canada has also focused on scaling up the use of electronic prescribing and other ehealth initiatives and recently committed CAD 300 million over five years to expand e-prescribing, increase EHR use and improve linkages between EHR systems, and improve patient access to health records. Through a project to support integrated service provision reform in Estonia, the government is harnessing its advanced digital capacity to improve the interoperability of registries and administrative datasets for individuals with needs for integrated care and vocational support. Efforts to improve the integration of digital tools have been accompanied by the introduction of performance-based financing to better incentivise integrated care.

Co-ordination between long-term care services delivered through social care, and health, poses an additional challenge to integration, particularly when health and social care are under the purview of different ministries. In Japan since 2018, co-ordination at the municipal level between home medical care and long-term care has been promoted through a programme funded by the long-term care insurance scheme, so that older people who require support from both medical and long-term care can continue to live at home until the end of their lives. In Norway, anybody requiring long-term health and social care services is entitled to an individual care plan, if they would like one. The patient and their family (next of kin) must be given the opportunity to be involved, if they wish to be.

Developing a holistic people-centred approach to health

Countries have in recent years scaled up a range of policies that promote or aim to strengthen people-centredness, across all five dimensions important to the health system. There is widespread recognition of both the importance of moving towards a people-centred approach, and an understanding of many of the barriers to doing so, including health systems fragmentation, skills mismatch, poor health literacy, and power imbalances that can detract from informed and active participation on the part of the patient. At the same time, many of the policies that have contributed to advancing the transition towards people-centredness have been developed primarily aimed at other goals – such as improving efficiency or quality – that are critical to achieving a high-performing health system, but not implemented in the interest of people-centredness per se. As such, many measures may not take into account their broader role in achieving people-centred health and systems. In other words, the development and delivery of many people-centred policies often remains fragmented.

There is a clear need to more deeply institutionalise the impact on people-centredness as a key parameter across health policy making, so that trade-offs can be made more apparent and a better balance can be achieved among policy objectives, such as efficiency, health security, or people-centredness. The OECD Framework and Scorecard for People-Centred Health Systems aims to contribute to the policy making process and to provide tools for countries to examine and evaluate such impacts. Far from being a definitive or all-encompassing framework for health policy, it is intended to shed more light on the policy issues surrounding health system from the perspective of the people.

The response to the global COVID-19 pandemic provides a good example of the application of the People-Centred Health Systems framework to a concrete and urgent policy need, underscoring the fragmented approach to people-centred policy making. In some ways, measures taken to contain the pandemic have furthered long-held goals of people-centred health systems, such as the adoption of digital tools and teleconsultations that have facilitated patient choice, or the promotion of multidisciplinary teams and expansion of responsibilities taken by certain primary care practitioners, including community pharmacists. At the same time, the speed of the response meant that patient voices were not included as systematically as a person-centred response would warrant, and many of the measures adopted – most notably infection control policies adopted in hospitals and long-term care facilities – went against the expressed wishes of patients and their families.

A lack of thorough measurement across the five dimensions of people-centred health systems underscores the reality that countries have further to go to delivering systematically people-centred policies, across sectors, services, and levels of the health system. Benchmarking across the five dimensions of the OECD Framework has highlighted that while certain countries appear to perform relatively strongly across the different dimensions of people-centredness, very few countries perform uniformly well across voice, choice, co-production, integration and respectfulness in orienting their health systems to be people centred. Moreover, data availability across all measures and dimensions by country remains inconsistent. The lack of available data to measure progress across all five dimensions underscores how far many countries have to go to better embedding people-centredness as a key actionable principle throughout their health systems. All countries have room to improve the people-centredness of their health systems.

References

Aalto, A. et al. (2018), "What patients think about choice in healthcare? A study on primary care services in Finland", *Scandinavian Journal of Public Health*, Vol. 46/4, pp. 463-470, http://dx.doi.org/10.1177/1403494817731488. [23]

Aujoulat, I., W. d'Hoore and A. Deccache (2007), *Patient empowerment in theory and practice: Polysemy or cacophony?*, http://dx.doi.org/10.1016/j.pec.2006.09.008. [27]

Australian Digital Health Agency (2021), *My Health Record: The Big Picture*. [32]

Barker, W. et al. (1985), "Geriatric Consultation Teams in Acute Hospitals: Impact on Back-up of Elderly Patients", *Journal of the American Geriatrics Society*, http://dx.doi.org/10.1111/j.1532-5415.1985.tb07153.x. [49]

Blomqvist, P. (2004), "The Choice Revolution: Privatization of Swedish Welfare Services in the 1990s", *Social Policy and Administration*, Vol. 38/2, pp. 139-155, http://dx.doi.org/10.1111/j.1467-9515.2004.00382.x. [18]

Boivin, A. et al. (2014), "Involving patients in setting priorities for healthcare improvement: A cluster randomized trial", *Implementation Science*, Vol. 9/1, http://dx.doi.org/10.1186/1748-5908-9-24. [14]

Bombard, Y. et al. (2018), *Engaging patients to improve quality of care: A systematic review*, BioMed Central Ltd., http://dx.doi.org/10.1186/s13012-018-0784-z. [11]

Boote, J., R. Telford and C. Cooper (2002), *Consumer involvement in health research: a review and research agenda*, http://www.elsevier.com/locate/healthpol. [5]

Brett, J. et al. (2014), "Mapping the impact of patient and public involvement on health and social care research: A systematic review", *Health Expectations*, Vol. 17/5, pp. 637-650, http://dx.doi.org/10.1111/j.1369-7625.2012.00795.x. [7]

Burgess, D. et al. (2008), "The association between perceived discrimination and underutilization of needed medical and mental health care in a multi-ethnic community sample", *Journal of Health Care for the Poor and Underserved*, Vol. 19/3, pp. 894-911, http://dx.doi.org/10.1353/hpu.0.0063. [40]

Caron-Flinterman, J., J. Broerse and J. Bunders (2005), "The experiential knowledge of patients: A new resource for biomedical research?", *Social Science and Medicine*, Vol. 60/11, pp. 2575-2584, http://dx.doi.org/10.1016/j.socscimed.2004.11.023. [4]

Conklin, A., Z. Morris and E. Nolte (2015), "What is the evidence base for public involvement in health-care policy?: Results of a systematic scoping review", *Health Expectations*, Vol. 18/2, pp. 153-165, http://dx.doi.org/10.1111/hex.12038. [1]

Costa-Font, J. and V. Zigante (2016), "The choice agenda in European health systems: the role of middle-class demands", *Public Money and Management*, Vol. 36/6, pp. 409-416, http://dx.doi.org/10.1080/09540962.2016.1206748. [16]

Crawford, M. et al. (2002), "Systematic review of involving patients in the planning and development of health care", *British Medical Journal*, Vol. 325/7375, pp. 1263-1265, http://dx.doi.org/10.1136/bmj.325.7375.1263. [12]

De Cruppé, W. and M. Geraedts (2017), "Hospital choice in Germany from the patient's perspective: A cross-sectional study", *BMC Health Services Research*, Vol. 17/1, http://dx.doi.org/10.1186/s12913-017-2712-3. [21]

Farin, E., L. Gramm and E. Schmidt (2013), "The patient-physician relationship in patients with chronic low back pain as a predictor of outcomes after rehabilitation", *Journal of Behavioral Medicine*, Vol. 36/3, pp. 246-258, http://dx.doi.org/10.1007/s10865-012-9419-z. [38]

Fujisawa, R. and N. Klazinga (2017), "Measuring patient experiences (PREMS): Progress made by the OECD and its member countries between 2006 and 2016", *OECD Health Working Papers*, No. 102, OECD Publishing, Paris, https://dx.doi.org/10.1787/893a07d2-en. [46]

Keers, J. et al. (2004), "Diabetes rehabilitation: Development and first results of a Multidisciplinary Intensive Education Program for patients with prolonged self-management difficulties", *Patient Education and Counseling*, Vol. 52/2, pp. 151-157, http://dx.doi.org/10.1016/S0738-3991(03)00019-3. [30]

Khan, R. and K. Socha-Dietrich (2018), "Investing in medication adherence improves health outcomes and health system efficiency: Adherence to medicines for diabetes, hypertension, and hyperlipidaemia", *OECD Health Working Papers*, No. 105, OECD Publishing, Paris, https://dx.doi.org/10.1787/8178962c-en. [34]

Kim, S., S. Kaplowitz and M. Johnston (2004), "The effects of physician empathy on patient satisfaction and compliance", *Evaluation and the Health Professions*, Vol. 27/3, pp. 237-251, http://dx.doi.org/10.1177/0163278704267037. [37]

Lako, C. and P. Rosenau (2009), "Demand-driven care and hospital choice. Dutch health policy toward demand-driven care: Results from a survey into hospital choice", *Health Care Analysis*, Vol. 17/1, pp. 20-35, http://dx.doi.org/10.1007/s10728-008-0093-9. [20]

Landeiro, F., J. Leal and A. Gray (2016), "The impact of social isolation on delayed hospital discharges of older hip fracture patients and associated costs", *Osteoporosis International*, http://dx.doi.org/10.1007/s00198-015-3293-9. [47]

Lee, C., S. Ayers and J. Jacobs Kronenfeld (2009), "The Association between Perceived Provider Discrimination, Health Care Utilization, and Health Status in Racial and Ethnic Minorities", *Ethnic Discrimination*, http://www.commonwealthfund.org. [41]

Lloyd, K. and J. White (2011), "Democratizing clinical research", *Nature*, Vol. 474, pp. 277-278, https://doi.org/10.1038/474277a. [9]

Loh, A. et al. (2007), "The impact of patient participation on adherence and clinical outcome in primary care of depression", *Patient Education and Counseling*, Vol. 65/1, pp. 69-78, http://dx.doi.org/10.1016/j.pec.2006.05.007. [28]

Longo, F. et al. (2019), "Does hospital competition improve efficiency? The effect of the patient choice reform in England", *Health Economics (United Kingdom)*, Vol. 28/5, pp. 618-640, http://dx.doi.org/10.1002/hec.3868. [19]

Moreira, L. (2018), "Health literacy for people-centred care: Where do OECD countries stand?", *OECD Health Working Papers*, No. 107, OECD Publishing, Paris, https://dx.doi.org/10.1787/d8494d3a-en. [33]

Oderkirk, J. (2017), "Readiness of electronic health record systems to contribute to national health information and research", *OECD Health Working Papers*, No. 99, OECD Publishing, Paris, https://dx.doi.org/10.1787/9e296bf3-en. [52]

OECD (2021), *Health at a Glance 2021: OECD Indicators*, OECD Publishing, Paris, https://doi.org/10.1787/ae3016b9-en. [25]

OECD (2020), *Realising the Potential of Primary Health Care*, OECD Health Policy Studies, OECD Publishing, Paris, https://dx.doi.org/10.1787/a92adee4-en. [51]

OECD (2019), *Health at a Glance 2019: OECD Indicators*, OECD Publishing, Paris, https://doi.org/10.1787/4dd50c09-en. [24]

OECD (2019), *Health in the 21st Century: Putting Data to Work for Stronger Health Systems*, OECD Health Policy Studies, OECD Publishing, Paris, https://dx.doi.org/10.1787/e3b23f8e-en. [31]

OECD (2018), *Feasibility Study on Health Workforce Skills Assessment: Supporting health workers achieve person-centred care*, OECD, Paris, https://www.oecd.org/els/health-systems/Feasibility-Study-On-Health-Workforce-Skills-Assessment-Feb2018.pdf. [35]

OECD (2016), *Health Systems Characteristics Survey*, https://qdd.oecd.org/subject.aspx?Subject=hsc. [43]

OECD (2016), *Health Workforce Policies in OECD Countries: Right Jobs, Right Skills, Right Places*, OECD Health Policy Studies, OECD Publishing, Paris, https://dx.doi.org/10.1787/9789264239517-en. [36]

Palumbo, R. (2016), *Contextualizing co-production of health care: a systematic literature review*, Emerald Group Publishing Ltd., http://dx.doi.org/10.1108/IJPSM-07-2015-0125. [44]

Rojas-García, A. et al. (2017), "Impact and experiences of delayed discharge: A mixed-studies systematic review", *Health Expectations*, Vol. 21/1, pp. 41-56, http://dx.doi.org/10.1111/hex.12619. [48]

Ryan, A., G. Gee and D. Griffith (2008), "The effects of perceived discrimination on diabetes management", *Journal of Health Care for the Poor and Underserved*, Vol. 19/1, pp. 149-163, http://dx.doi.org/10.1353/hpu.2008.0005. [42]

Sacristán, J. et al. (2016), *Patient involvement in clinical research: Why, when, and how*, Dove Medical Press Ltd., http://dx.doi.org/10.2147/PPA.S104259. [10]

Santos, R., H. Gravelle and C. Propper (2017), "Does Quality Affect Patients' Choice of Doctor? Evidence from England", *Economic Journal*, Vol. 127/600, pp. 445-494, http://dx.doi.org/10.1111/ecoj.12282. [17]

Schölvinck, A., C. Pittens and J. Broerse (2020), "Patient involvement in agenda-setting processes in health research policy: A boundary work perspective", *Science and Public Policy*, http://dx.doi.org/10.1093/scipol/scaa001. [6]

Shepperd, S. et al. (2013), *Discharge planning from hospital to home*, John Wiley & Sons, Ltd, Chichester, UK, http://dx.doi.org/10.1002/14651858.cd000313.pub4. [50]

Simpson, E. and A. House (2002), "Involving users in the delivery and evaluation of mental health services: Systematic review", *British Medical Journal*, Vol. 325/7375, pp. 1265-1268, http://dx.doi.org/10.1136/bmj.325.7375.1265. [13]

Slawomirski, L., A. Auraaen and N. Klazinga (2017), "The economics of patient safety : Strengthening a value-based approach to reducing patient harm at national level", *OECD Health Working Papers*, No. 96, OECD Publishing, Paris, https://dx.doi.org/10.1787/5a9858cd-en. [15]

Stovell, D. et al. (2016), "Shared treatment decision-making and empowerment related outcomes in psychosis: Systematic review and meta-analysis", *British Journal of Psychiatry*, Vol. 209/1, pp. 23-28, http://dx.doi.org/10.1192/bjp.bp.114.158931. [29]

Taneda, K. (2016), "多機種チームをまとめ、患者の多様なニーズに応える"地域包括ケア*コンシェルジュ"の育成", *病院*, Vol. 75/6, pp. 414-419, https://doi.org/10.11477/mf.1541210112. [45]

Thurston, W. et al. (2005), "Public participation in regional health policy: A theoretical framework", *Health Policy*, http://dx.doi.org/10.1016/j.healthpol.2004.11.013. [3]

Trummer, U. et al. (2006), "Does physician-patient communication that aims at empowering patients improve clinical outcome?. A case study", *Patient Education and Counseling*, Vol. 61/2, pp. 299-306, http://dx.doi.org/10.1016/j.pec.2005.04.009. [26]

Victoor, A. et al. (2016), "Why patients may not exercise their choice when referred for hospital care. An exploratory study based on interviews with patients", *Health Expectations*, Vol. 19/3, pp. 667-678, http://dx.doi.org/10.1111/hex.12224. [22]

Wait, S. and E. Nolte (2006), "Public involvement policies in health: exploring their conceptual basis.", *Health economics, policy, and law*, Vol. 1/Pt 2, pp. 149-162, http://dx.doi.org/10.1017/S174413310500112X. [2]

Wilson, P. et al. (2015), "ReseArch with Patient and Public invOlvement: a RealisT evaluation – the RAPPORT study", *Health Services and Delivery Research*, Vol. 3/38, pp. 1-176, http://dx.doi.org/10.3310/hsdr03380. [8]

Zachariae, R. et al. (2003), "Association of perceived physician communication style with patient satisfaction, distress, cancer-related self-efficacy, and perceived control over the disease", *British Journal of Cancer*, Vol. 88/5, pp. 658-665, http://dx.doi.org/10.1038/sj.bjc.6600798. [39]

3 The COVID-19 pandemic has made people-centredness even more urgent

This chapter applies the OECD Framework for People-Centred Health Systems to the COVID-19 response pursued by health systems and governments across OECD countries to consider the extent to which the policies put in place to fight the pandemic were people-centred. It finds that the policies pursued to contain and mitigate the pandemic largely did not prioritise – and in many cases conflicted with – the key principles of people-centredness. The response to the COVID-19 pandemic has underscored that many principles of people-centredness remain poorly institutionalised within health systems policy making. It further argues that while the urgency of the pandemic sometimes necessitated responses that deprioritised people-centredness, a more person-centred approach to certain challenges raised may in fact have helped to avert some of the difficulties countries continue to face nearly two years into the pandemic.

The rapid development of COVID-19 into a global pandemic over the past 15 months has dramatically tested health systems globally. In many countries, efforts to contain the spread of the virus have led to the implementation of bold and often extraordinary policies, many of which have turned usual medical and social practice on its head. Within this rapidly changing context, seeking people-centredness in the response may seem a secondary priority to the immense task of tackling the epidemic. However, this would take a myopic view of the crisis. A person-centred approach is essential to an effective COVID-19 response in OECD countries.

Scaling up a government response to the pressing needs of COVID-19 requires also attending to the regular needs of patients seeking care and support. In some cases, the policies adopted to address the COVID-19 outbreak have created serious challenges to high-quality care for several other conditions, such as diabetes (Chudasama et al., 2020[1]) and cancer care (The Lancet Oncology, 2021[2]). Reports from many countries have suggested that time-sensitive care is sometimes being delayed or forgone during the crisis (OECD/European Union, 2020[3]; OECD, 2021[4]). It is critical that responses balance attention to the current crisis without sacrificing the other needs of health systems users.

Despite the difficulties faced by health systems during the COVID-19 pandemic, a number of positive lessons can also be drawn from the speed at which health systems have been able to adapt their ways of working and introduce new policies, practices and flexibilities, often in the face of considerable pressures. Some longstanding barriers to people-centredness can be quickly addressed while others are much more unyielding. For example, telemedicine has been accelerated to an extent that was unthinkable before the pandemic.

The need for fast decisions often reduced patients' voice during the pandemic, and patient involvement and participation has been underutilised

Prior to the COVID-19 pandemic, policy commitments were made to broaden patient and public involvement and improve shared decision in health systems. However, the need to accelerate decision and implementation of policies to contain the spread of COVID-19 and prepare providers care for acute patients has often come at the expense of patient voice and shared decision-making (Richards and Scowcroft, 2020[5]; Köther, Siebenhaar and Alpers, 2021[6]).

As the response to the pandemic evolves, renewed appeals have been made to bring increases in public and patient involvement, as a way to achieve several important goals including: to increase public trust and confidence in health systems responses; facilitate public compliance with containment measures; identify better treatments and new approaches to care delivery, including those for vulnerable and underserved populations; and overcome vaccine hesitancy (Murphy et al., 2020[7]). The pandemic also made clear the need to better institutionalise mechanisms to include patient voice in more rapid policy responses, such as the COVID-19 pandemic, as a way of ensuring the quality of care, improving decisions, managing the politics of expert advice in times of uncertainty (Moore and MacKenzie, 2020[8]).

The institutionalisation of patient participation and involvement can serve as a platform for the interaction between patients and health care authorities, including during times of emergency or crisis (Dobiášová, Kotherová and Numerato, 2021[9]). However, meaningful examples of patient involvement and participation in the pandemic still seem to be limited. According to a survey conducted with 57 patient organisations in Europe, 63% of respondents indicated that there was no patient involvement in the management of the pandemic at all, and only 12% of responding organisations agreed that there was good patient involvement in their country's COVID-19 crisis taskforce (European Patients Forum, 2021[10]).

Digital access to primary health care consultations has partially mitigated the reduction of patient choice as in-person consultations fell dramatically

The growing use of digital tools in health systems offers the opportunity to overcome certain choice barriers, including access. The rapid expansion of telemedicine tools during the COVID-19 pandemic across the globe has demonstrated the enormous potential of virtual health services to overcome access-related barriers to care (Bhaskar et al., 2020[11]). Nowhere has this been more evident than in the rapid scale-up of digital tools for health care.

In many countries, timelines for the roll out of telemedicine services and other digital approaches that were previously counted in years were shortened into a span of mere months (Marin, 2020[12]). Many countries such as Austria, Belgium, the Czech Republic, Estonia and Korea introduced or hastened the scale-up of remote consultations during the pandemic, while other countries that already allowed telemedicine services, such as France, Luxembourg, Poland, and the United States, rapidly expanded reimbursement for these services (OECD/European Union, 2020[3]). Some of the changes put in place to facilitate digital health delivery were initially temporary, such as the addition of telehealth services to the Medicare Benefits Scheme in Australia, but underpin broader plans to transition towards a more comprehensive policy of virtual care. In Portugal, a collaboration between the health care call centre SNS24 and a telehealth platform developed during the pandemic (Trace-COVID-19) created a system of triage and referral to identify the most appropriate setting for patients.

Nonetheless, not all barriers that impact patient choice can be overcome with digital solutions alone, and there is some evidence that the rise of telemedicine was not sufficient to compensate for the dramatic reduction of in-person consultations. A large study of insured populations in the United States covering over 36 million people found that total in-person ambulatory contacts decreased from 1.63 contacts per person in March-June 2019 to 1.02 contacts per person in March-June 2020, while telehealth ambulatory contacts per person rose from 0.01 to 0.32 in the same period (Weiner et al., 2021[13]). Furthermore, populations living in least socially advantages areas were less likely to have access to telemedicine when compared to wealthier populations (Figure 3.1). Given that the study data refer to insured populations only, the results may be even less favourable to uninsured people. Data for the second semester of 2020 indicate a rebound in the levels of in-person consultations (Mehrotra et al., 2021[14]).

Similar patterns of expansion of telemedicine were observed in other countries. In France, for example, teleconsultations reached 27% of total consultations at the height of the lockdown in 2020 (Richardson et al., 2020[15]). In Norway, the proportion of general practitioner consultations that were performed remotely reached a peak of 60% between 16 and 22 March 2020, then declined to 25% in the last week of March 2020, a level which was maintained for several months (Johnsen et al., 2021[16]).

Telemedical services were not the only digital tools expanded by health systems during the pandemic. In Korea, vaccine availability was monitored using online and app-based reporting systems to keep track of the number of remaining doses across hospitals, and promote equity and up-take of the vaccine. Mobile apps were also developed to keep track of the public distribution of face masks.

The expansion of telemedicine however, affected specialties in a different manner, and digital technology is not able to replace services that require physicial interventions, such as surgeries or diagnostic exams that require direct physical examinations. A study of insured populations in the United States found strong reductions were observed from January-February to March-April 2020 in diagnostic procedures such as colonoscopies, mammograms, hemoglobin A1C tests, and vaccines; some types of non-elective surgeries, includingangioplasties, elective surgeries, and the use of mangetic ressonance imaging from – the point at which the pandemic had begun to spread aroudn the world (Whaley et al., 2020[17]).

Figure 3.1. In the United States, populations living in less socially advantaged areas had less access to telemedicine

Total ambulatory encounters per person (in-person and telehealth) in March-June 2019 and March-June 2020, and share of telehealth encounters in March-June 2020, by level of deprivation of place of residence in the United States

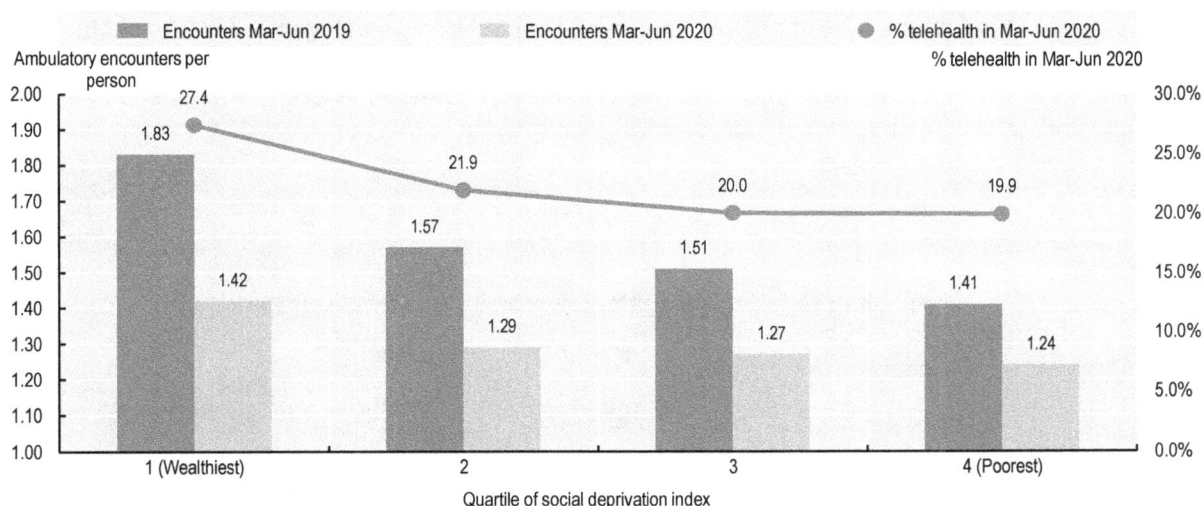

Note: From March to June 2019, telehealth ambulatory encounters were 0.3% of the total for all four quartiles of social deprivation index.
Source: Authors preparation with data from Weiner et al. (2021[13]), "In-Person and Telehealth Ambulatory Contacts and Costs in a Large US Insured Cohort Before and During the COVID-19 Pandemic", https://doi.org/10.1001/jamanetworkopen.2021.2618.

Engaging people has been critical for pandemic containment efforts, but a balance between incentives and restrictions is still needed

As part of the containment policies introduced in the first semester of 2020, severe restrictions in the circulation of people were adopted and levels of population compliance were high. A study of 52 countries found that on 11 March 2020, population mobility had dropped 63% from its baseline (Nouvellet et al., 2021[18]).

People's engagement was also necessary for the adoption of other preventive behaviours, such as the use of facemasks. When the virus first appeared, the predominant modes of transmission were initially unclear, but evidence emerged to suggest that the main mode of transmission was through respiratory droplets and that the use of facemasks was an effective way to prevent transmission (Howard et al., 2021[19]). Countries gradually adopted mandates or recommendations for the use of facemasks in public spaces: during 2020, the first mandates and requirements for facemasks usage in public were introduced in Chile, Italy, and Germany in early April; in France, Korea, and Spain in early May; in the Netherlands in early June; in Canada, Costa Rica, and the United Kingdom in late June; in Australia in late July; and in Denmark in late August, albeit with regional variation in some of these countries, notably in Spain, the United Kingdom and the United States (Hale et al., 2021[20]).

Results of large international studies conducted with Facebook users have provided some insights about the usage of facemasks, even though these need to be interpreted with caution as the data represents only social media users and may not be representative of the general population (Perrotta et al., 2021[21]; Fan et al., 2020[22]; Badillo-Goicoechea et al., 2021[23]). While mandates and recommendations did have an effect in the uptake of facemask usage, many other factors impact the response across countries. Some countries, including Japan and Korea, had persistently high rates of reported facemask usage, remaining well above 90% throughout the pandemic. Other countries, including Costa Rica and Spain, saw a rapid uptake in facemask usage in May and June 2020 and have maintained high levels of usage of over 90%; in Canada and France, mask usage rates have been between 80% and 90%. In the United Kingdom, the highest rates were between October 2020 and July 2021, and have fallen in subsequent months. In Australia, around 30% of the population reported usage between August 2020 and July 2021, with usage rising sharply thereafter before more recently declining. In Denmark, reported facemask usage has mostly remained below the 50% mark, with the highest rates observed between November 2020 and June 2021 (Figure 3.2). Some of the variation in face mask usage is likely related to the country's guidelines and rules concerning use: in France, for example, face masks remain required in indoor buildings such as shops, while obligatory face coverings were lifted in the United Kingdom in mid-summer 2021, though have since been re-imposed in some settings.

Figure 3.2. Self-reported facemask usage, 7-day averages between May 2020-November 2021

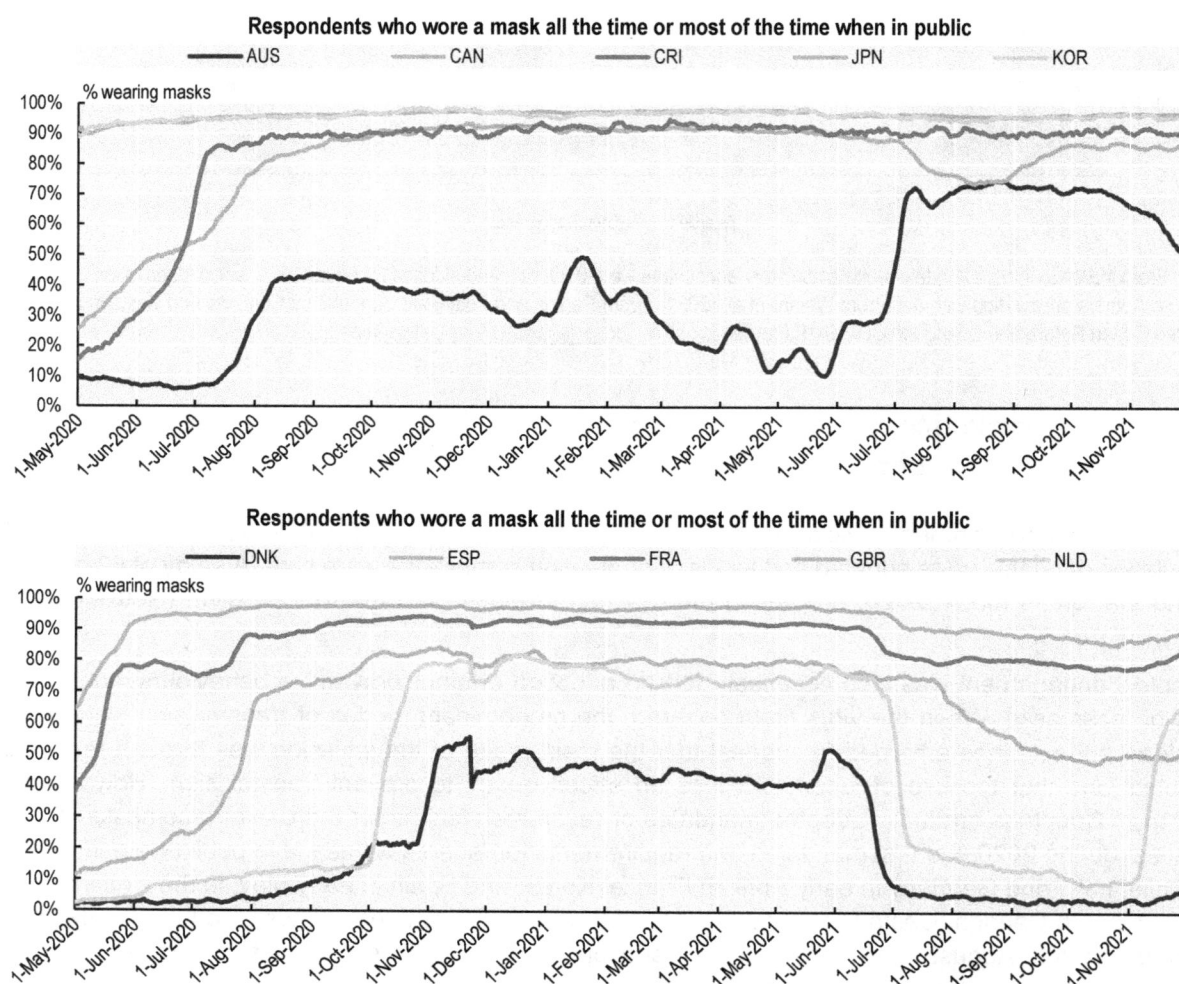

Respondents who wore a mask all the time or most of the time when in public

Respondents who wore a mask all the time or most of the time when in public

Note: Results from 64 572 869 responses collected between 23 April 2020 and 29 November 2021 from Facebook users in 113 countries and territories by "The University of Maryland Social Data Science Center Global COVID-19 Trends and Impact Survey, in partnership with Facebook".
Source: Fan et al. (2020[22]), The University of Maryland Social Data Science Center Global COVID-19 Trends and Impact Survey, in partnership with Facebook, https://covidmap.umd.edu/api.html.

While the evidence still confirms that the use of facemasks is important to prevent infections (Li and Sun, 2021[24]; Howard et al., 2021[19]; Liao et al., 2021[25]), immunisation became the main policy tool to contain the pandemic as soon as vaccines became available in late 2020 and early 2021. As countries began to expand their vaccination programmes, ensuring people understand and agree with the new vaccines has been critical to reach the high levels of population vaccination that are needed for herd protection given the highly contagious nature of SARS-CoV-2 (Fontanet and Cauchemez, 2020[26]). However, after the initial supply and logistical challenges were addressed across OECD countries, persistence in vaccination hesitancy among a fraction of the population has been a roadblock in reaching universal immunisation. Bringing people on board is further critical given the likelihood that vaccination against COVID-19 will not be a one-off occurrence, but will rather require some booster doses in addition to their initial immunisation in at least the medium term.

Across 11 OECD countries in December 2020, when the vast majority of the people had not yet been vaccinated, between 23% and 60% of the population indicated that they would not get a COVID-19 vaccine if it were made available to them (Figure 3.3). Vaccine hesitancy dropped somewhat by the end of February 2021, when between 13% and 35% of the people across the eleven countries indicated that they would not get a vaccine. However, as vaccination programmes expanded, by late April 2021, the proportion of unvaccinated people who were unwilling to receive a vaccine grew in several countries, reaching 29% in Germany, 34% in Australia, 42% in France, and 54% in the United States.

Figure 3.3. Attitudes on COVID-19 vaccination in 11 OECD countries, Aug 2020-April 2021

"If a vaccine for COVID-19 were available to me, I would get it"

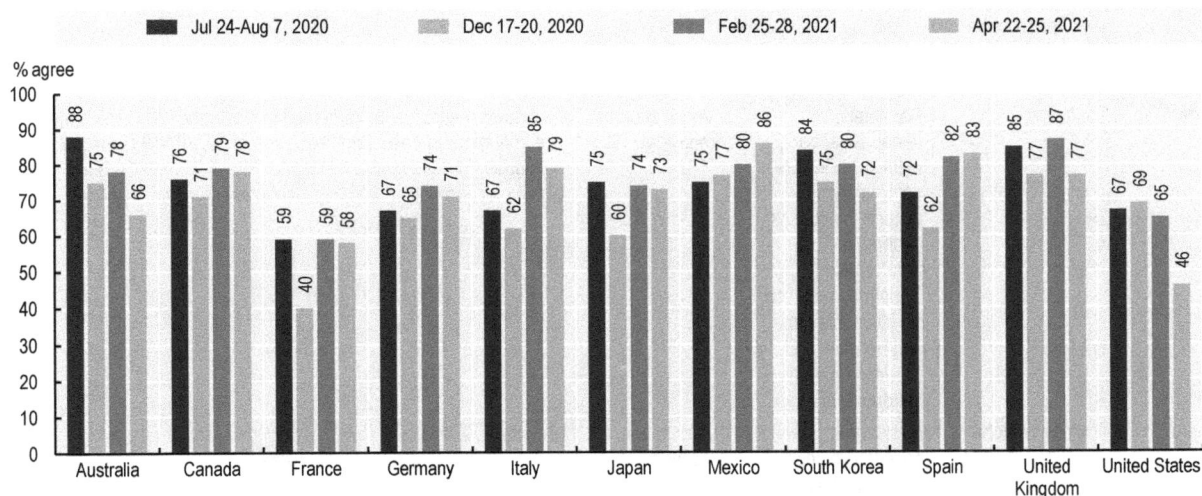

Note: April 2021 only among those reporting they had not received the vaccine.
Source: Ipsos (2021[27]), COVID-19 Vaccination Intent. Ipsos survey for The World Economic Forum.

Misinformation appears to have played a role in fuelling vaccine hesitancy, even before the COVID-19 pandemic. A study in Italy found an association between the dissemination of fake news and misinformation about immunisation in social networks in 2012 and a decrease in child immunisation rates (Carrieri, Madio and Principe, 2019[28]). More recent studies have also discussed the association of misinformation on social media and COVID-19 vaccine hesitancy (Garett and Young, 2021[29]; Lockyer et al., 2021[30]). These concerns illustrate the challenge that countries face in rapidly scaling up a population-wide vaccination campaign and underscores the importance of good communication and co-production between health systems and the broader population (OECD, 2021[31]).

As the pandemic persisted into the second half of 2021, many OECD countries still struggled to convince a sizable minority of their citizens to be vaccinated, and a plateauing effect in vaccination coverage was observed in several OECD countries, including Austria, the Czech Republic, Germany, Hungary, Israel, Switzerland, the United States and others. This has created a major roadblock in efforts to prevent the further spread of the COVID-19 virus, particularly given the onset of the more virulent Delta variant, and the looming threat of further highly infectious variants such as Omicron. In November 2021, even countries where a majority of the eligible population had been vaccinated still had sizeable numbers of people susceptible to the disease, and a sharp resurgence of cases was observed in many European countries.

One measure taken by the majority of OECD countries to discourage COVID-19 transmission and incentivise vaccination has been the introduction of COVID-19 'passes' intended to restrict access to certain public venues to people who fulfil requirements, often related to vaccination, testing, or recovery from COVID-19. Across the 38 OECD countries, by early December 2021, over three-fifths (24 countries) had implemented national COVID-19 pass requirements, while a further ten countries had introduced voluntary, partial, or regionally based COVID-19 passes (Table 3.1). Only four countries had not introduced any form of COVID-19 pass control to restrict access in at least some public spaces. Despite their coercive nature and an arguable restriction of individual liberty, these measures – introduced in many countries to incentivise vaccination – have received broad popular support, indicating a possible balance between incentives and coercion as a way forward through the pandemic.

Table 3.1. Status of COVID-19 pass requirements in OECD countries, early December 2021

Country	Has a COVID-19 pass been implemented?	Locations applicable	Requirements	Further information
Australia	No			
Austria	Yes	For hotels, restaurants, bars, nightclubs, leisure centres, gyms, cultural institutions (cinemas, theatres etc.), Christmas markets, ski lifts/cable cars and body-related services (such as hairdressers)	Vaccination or recovery	Lockdown measures implemented in November 2021 following a rise in number of cases; domestic use of COVID-19 certificate continues (Federal Ministry of Social Affairs, Health Care and Consumer Protection, 2021[32]; Schengeninfonews, 2021[33])
Belgium	Yes, regionally	restaurants, gyms, hospitals, cafes, discos, cultural venues hosting more than 50 people, optional for residential care facilities of vulnerable people (mandatory in Wallonia)	Vaccination, recovery or test	(Bencharif, 2021[34])
Canada	Yes, regionally	Mainly, for international and domestic travel	Vaccination	Each province in Canada may use the certificate in a different manner (Al Jazeera, 2021[35])
Chile	Yes	Public venues, restaurants, bars etc. and long-distance travel on public transport	Vaccination	Booster doses will be required from 1 Jan 2022 for those that have +6 months of full vaccination (Government of Chile, 2021[36])

Country	Has a COVID-19 pass been implemented?	Locations applicable	Requirements	Further information
Colombia	Yes	Public venues, restaurants, bars, cinemas and other commerce	Vaccination	(Terra Colombia, 2021[37])
Costa Rica	Yes	Capacity of some businesses and public spaces limited to 50% if not accepting only vaccinated clients (hotels, restaurants, bars, casinos, museums, gyms etc.)	Vaccination	From 8 Jan 2022, vaccine certificates will be required to enter certain venues; first country to mandate COVID-19 vaccine for children; Mandate for all state workers (BBC, 2021[38])
Czech Republic	Yes	Public events and services	Vaccination (and possibly recovery)	(de Goeij, 2021[39])
Denmark	Yes	Bars, restaurants, cafes and nightclubs; cultural activities, churches with more than 200 participants (indoors), courses, conferences	Vaccination, recovery or test	Denmark had previously implemented and abolished requirements associated with its Coronapas, and has reinstated the pass (Nationalt Kommunikations Partnerskab COVID-19, 2021[40])
Estonia	Yes	Restaurants, gyms, hospitals, cafes, discos, cultural venues, public saunas and pools	Vaccination, recovery or test	(Kriss.EE Government Communication Unit, 2021[41])
Finland	Yes, optional (with restrictions)	Restaurants, cafes, bars, amusement parks, museums, spas, pools and other public venues.	Vaccination, recovery or test	Passes are introduced on a voluntary basis by each establishment, but restrictions apply to those not willing (prohibition on serving alcohol after 5pm, e.g.) Restrictions may vary between regions. (Kanta Services, 2021[42])
France	Yes	Wide range of use, most of public venues, including also long distance travel	Vaccination, recovery or test	Third dose of vaccine being rolled out as a requirement to keep the passe sanitaire (El Pais, 2021[43])
Germany	Yes	Indoor hospitality venues, stores (excluded basic necessities)	Vaccination and recovery (some few regions also accept tests)	Additional restriction for the non-vaccinated (El Pais, 2021[43])
Greece	Yes	Restaurants, cafes, bars, cinemas, theatres, gyms	Vaccination, recovery (test depending on venue, more limited)	Third dose of vaccine to be introduced for the certificate First country in Europe to mandate vaccines for over 60 (Politico.EU, 2021[44])
Hungary	Yes	Indoor sports and cultural events and outdoor events with +500 people	Vaccination	Vaccination mandate for health workers, could be extended to public sector employees (Reuters, 2021[45])
Iceland	No			There are restrictions on the number of people in public spaces, but no passport for vaccination/tests
Ireland	Yes	Gyms, leisure centres, hotel bars and restaurants	Vaccination or recovery	(Ireland Department of the Taoiseach, 2021[46])

Country	Has a COVID-19 pass been implemented?	Locations applicable	Requirements	Further information
Israel	Yes	Public spaces and events, no longer required for events of max 100 people indoors + for **work** in certain industries and professions	Vaccination and recovery	Israel has already introduced booster shots to all its population, and it's a requirement to keep the COVID-19 pass (Ministry of Health, 2021[47])
Italy	Yes	Most indoor facilities + events + long distance travel + **work**	Vaccination, recovery or test	In work restrictions, employees can be suspended and have their salaries withheld if they don't show a pass (El Pais, 2021[43])
Japan	Yes	Leisure in groups of more than 4, inter-city travel, some leisure activities and public spaces	Vaccination, tests	(Kyodo News, 2021[48])
South Korea	Yes	Restaurants, cafes, cinemas, gyms, saunas, discos and other public spaces	Vaccination	(Reuters, 2021[49])
Latvia	Yes	Large public venues and all services, except most basic needs	Vaccination, recovery or test	(Investment and Development Agency of Latvia, 2021[50])
Lithuania	Yes	Limits on the number of people in certain venues, which is higher in places that check COVID-19 passes	Vaccination, recovery or test	Booster shots to become mandatory in order to keep the travel vaccination certificate (Ministry of the Economy and Innovation of the Republic of Lithuania, 2021[51])
Luxembourg	Yes	Inside restaurants and bars, events of more than 10 people	Vaccination, recovery (test only in some occasions)	New legislation aims at restricting access to unvaccinated people to most non-essential venues. Also, plans to introduce the *pass sanitaire* at work (The Luxembourg Government, 2021[52])
Mexico	No			
Netherlands	Yes	Several indoor leisure activities and public venues (restaurants, bars, museums, cinemas, gyms etc.)	Vaccination, recovery or test	From Feb 2022 only people with booster shots will be able to maintain their COVID-19 pass (validity of 9 months) (Government of the Netherlands, 2021[53])
New Zealand	Yes, partially	Events, hospitality, close-contact services etc.	Vaccination	Optional in many venues, but with additional restrictions on number of people if verification is not applied (Ministry of Health, 2021[54])
Norway	Yes, optional and partially		Vaccination, recovery or test	Plans to introduce the corona pass (Reuters, 2021[55])
Poland	No			
Portugal	Yes	Restaurants, cafes, hotels, events, bars, discos, air and sea travel.	Vaccination, recovery or test	(GEO, 2021[56]; El Pais, 2021[43])
Slovak Republic	Yes	Events, restaurants, non-essential shop and shopping malls. Unvaccinated workers must get test regularly.	Vaccination	As of Dec 2021 under a curfew-based lockdown, which was recently extended. As of 10 Dec 2021, shops can open for vaccinated and recovered people (The Slovak Spectator, 2021[57])

Country	Has a COVID-19 pass been implemented?	Locations applicable	Requirements	Further information
Slovenia	Yes	Hospitality, restaurants, stores, public transport	Vaccination, recovery or test	Passes required from employees and users of public venues (Euractiv, 2021[58])
Spain	In preparation by regions	Most indoor hospitality venues, gyms, long term care facilities	Vaccination, recovery or test	Some regional governments are preparing the requirement of passes, Canary islands approved on a voluntary basis (El Pais, 2021[59])
Sweden	Yes, partially	Indoor events with more than 100 people.	Vaccination	Government has announced plans to introduce legislation aiming at extending the use of COVID-19 passes for restaurants and gyms (Government Offices of Sweden, 2021[60])
Switzerland	Yes	Restaurants, bars, indoor events, museums, libraries, gyms etc.	Vaccination, recovery or test	Referendum on the extension and use of COVID-19 passes received a strong backing from voters (France24, 2021[61])
Turkey	Yes, partially	Concerts, cinemas and theatres, for instance	Vaccination, tests	(Turkish Ministry of the Interior, 2021[62])
United Kingdom	Yes, partially	Nightclubs and large venues	Vaccination, recovery, tests	Wales requires for large events and nightclubs. Passes required in England for nightclubs and large venues (The Times, 2021[63]; El Pais, 2021[43])
United States	Partially			Vaccine certificates only being implemented in some states/cities, such as in New York. Only federal requirement concerns air travel (El Pais, 2021[43])

Containment efforts must consider the need for engaging people and providing support for the continuity of care, especially for people living with chronic conditions

Engaging people has been critical not only to achieve better results in mitigation efforts, but also to ensure ongoing care management. In addition to individual responsibility and adoption of preventive behaviours to contain the spread to the COVID-19 pandemic, another important aspect related to the COVID-19 pandemic was the continuity of care for chronic patients. In the opinion of over 200 health care professionals from 47 countries who participated in an online survey, diabetes care was by far the chronic condition most impacted by COVID-19 due to reduction of care (Chudasama et al., 2020[1]). In Portugal, hospital at home services that had been previously implemented were further strengthened during the pandemic, to encourage earlier hospital discharge and care integration that followed patients once they were home. Chronic disease commissions, including both health care professionals and patient representatives, helped to define strategies and action plans in response to care during the pandemic.

Emerging data points to the impacts of the pandemic on delays in care for chronic conditions, including cancer, as well as elective procedures. Across seven OECD countries with available data, the proportion of women aged 50-69 who were screened within the previous two years for breast cancer fell by 5 percentage points between 2019 and 2020, with reductions in screening particularly acute during the initial months of the pandemic (Figure 3.4). While the full impact of COVID-19 remains to be seen, delays in screening, diagnosis and treatment for conditions like cancer will likely have impacts on survival rates, further exacerbating the damaging legacy of the pandemic.

Figure 3.4. Breast cancer screening in previous two years

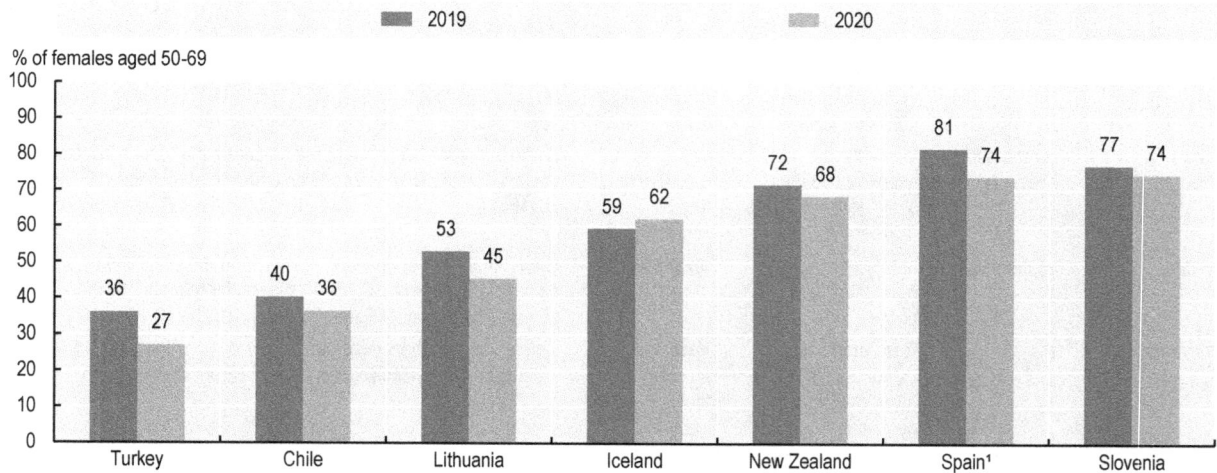

Note: Data for Spain is survey (not programme) data.
Source: OECD (2021[64]), *Health at a Glance 2021: OECD Indicators*, https://doi.org/10.1787/ae3016b9-en.

Non-urgent procedures also continue to be disrupted due to the pandemic. While delays in elective surgeries such as hip replacement may not have the same long-term impact on survival rates as delays in cancer care and treatment, postponements of elective surgery nonetheless have enormous impacts on the quality of life and well-being of the people who must live in discomfort or pain for longer than they had initially anticipated. Waiting times for hip replacement, knee replacement and cataract surgery all increased across the seven OECD countries with available data for 2020. On average, the median days spent on a waitlist before undergoing knee replacement surgery increased by 88 days in 2020 compared to 2019 for patients on surgery waiting lists, and 58 days for those on hip replacement surgery waiting lists (Figure 3.5).

Figure 3.5. Waiting times for hip replacement

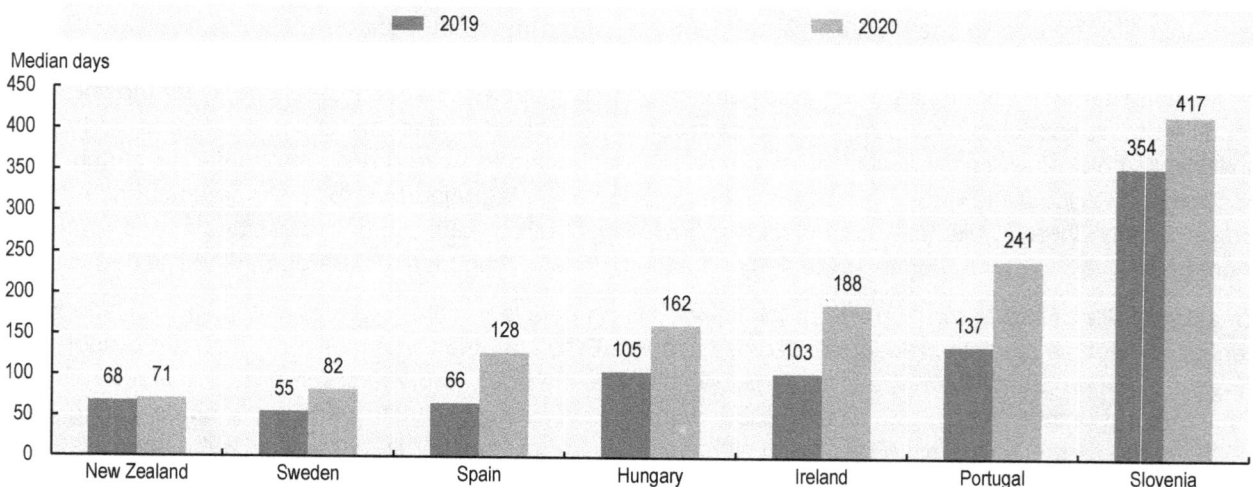

Source: OECD (2021[64]), *Health at a Glance 2021: OECD Indicators*, https://doi.org/10.1787/ae3016b9-en.

Digital technologies such as diabetes management apps can increase opportunities for co-production of health by patients and more agency in self-care through the capture of diabetes device data. However, not only is uptake of such technology relatively low, but their effectiveness also depends on the ability to share these data back to providers and integrate the information generated within patient's records to inform virtual care and improve care management (Gamble et al., 2020[65]). The pandemic has also offered a clear demonstration of the importance of harnessing available digital tools to facilitate better continuity of care. Electronic records in primary care, for example, offer a powerful tool to fight outbreaks. Some countries have harnessed the opportunity to identify and notify people at particularly high risk of complications, as identified through information recorded in electronic health and medical records, including people who are immunocompromised, have diabetes, and other chronic conditions. In many countries, digital tools have been employed to speed up access to COVID-19 testing results.

Strengthening multidisciplinary teams has helped to bolster co-ordination and integration of care, but information gaps remain a limiting factor

In many OECD countries, the scope of practice of community pharmacists has been expanded so that they can take on some of the tasks from doctors and allow them to spend their time more effectively on the most complex cases and minimise the number of medical consultations (OECD, 2021[4]). In Canada, Ireland, Portugal and the United States, for example, pharmacists have been allowed to extend prescriptions beyond what they were previously allowed to do and to prescribe certain medications. In the United States, community pharmacists have been authorised by the Food and Drug Administration to order and administer COVID-19 tests. In Scotland, community pharmacists performed an enhanced role during the COVID-19 pandemic, support more patients through the extension of Minor Ailment Service (MAS) to reduce the burden across the NHS and ensure patients continue to get the necessary medicines.

Community health workers have a role to play during the COVID-19 pandemic to ensure patients access to needed care. Community health workers who are integrated into primary health care services can also be beneficial during health emergencies. While community health workers provide opportunities to ensure that patients are connected to health care systems, they have not been mobilised as much as they could during the first wave of the COVID-19 pandemic. Only a few OECD countries made the best of community health workers to provide timely, accurate information about COVID-19 and ensure that people obtained access to care and support. The United States and the United Kingdom are two notable exceptions. In the United States, community health workers served as support in navigating the health care systems, and mitigating fear and correcting misinformation in disadvantaged communities (Peretz, Islam and Matiz, 2020[66]). The United Kingdom also proposed to use community health workers to provide support for vulnerable people (Haines et al., 2020[67]).

Information gaps limit the possibilities that different providers, teams, and professionals across the health system offer seamless, integrated care. In the case of COVID-19, it is critical that primary care providers are up to date about what happens to their patients in hospital settings, for example. Similarly, priority lists for vaccination can be drawn more efficiently if records are integrated and risk factors can be quickly identified by authorities who are planning the deployment of vaccines, just to give a few examples. For this to happen, health records need to be linked across the different databases of the health system. Record linkages enable the information value of individual datasets to grow, permitting connections between health care provided and the outcomes of that care over time; and permitting data within one dataset to be put into context with data from other sources (Oderkirk, 2021[68]). However, even though most countries are broadly using electronic health records, their health data infrastructure may limit the possibility that the data follow the patients across different levels of care, types of providers, and regions. Across 22 OECD countries, on average 83% of key national health datasets are available, but a much smaller percentage, 55% are regularly linked for research, statistics and monitoring (Figure 3.6).

Figure 3.6. Percentage of key national health datasets available and regularly linked for monitoring and research across 22 OECD countries and Singapore

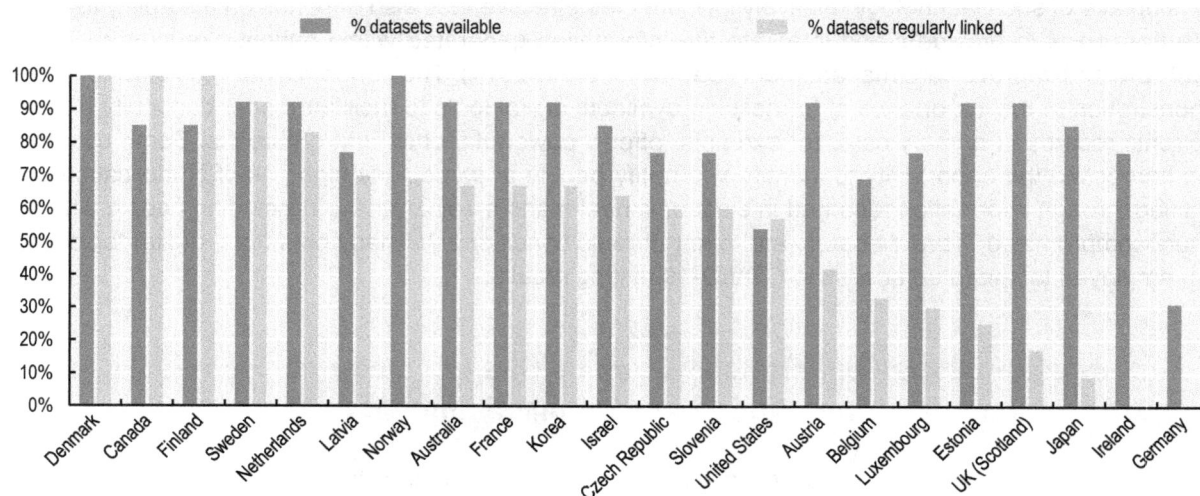

Source: Oderkirk (2021[68]), "Survey results: National health data infrastructure and governance", https://dx.doi.org/10.1787/55d24b5d-en.

Respectfulness was sometimes compromised to ensure patient and staff safety and must be urgently restored

Policies to promote patient safety have sometimes come at the expense of people-centred care – especially at the end of life. Many initial policy responses focused on containment in high-risk environments. Long term care (LTC) facilities and hospitals put in place policies highly restricting patient and family choice. LTC and end-of-life care has been particularly fraught, with family members and loved ones in some cases prevented from seeing sick family members in hospital or long-term care facilities, and funerals banned or restricted in many areas. In successfully implementing policies to fight COVID-19 that infringe on regular behaviours and undercut many rights people take for granted, other dimensions of people-centred care can become even more important.

Strongly institutionalising co-production and respectfulness, in particular, may be critical to ensuring populations trust and comply with these difficult decisions. Where health systems users and patients feel they have a say and are engaged in their health and are treated with respect, it may be easier to ensure buy-in when difficult policy measures must be put in place. In Poland, a free telephone patient hotline, serviced by the Patients' Rights Ombudsman, was established to collect complaints, problems, and other issues related to the COVID-19 pandemic.

In some cases, matters of trust may be beyond the control of health systems and health policy makers. Broader trust in government, including how the government has responded to the social crisis engendered by the COVID-19 pandemic, can colour how populations see the health systems response as much as the actual response itself. Across 36 OECD countries, fewer than half of people indicated they trusted their government in 2020 (OECD, 2020[69]).

Figure 3.7 Trust in government in OECD countries

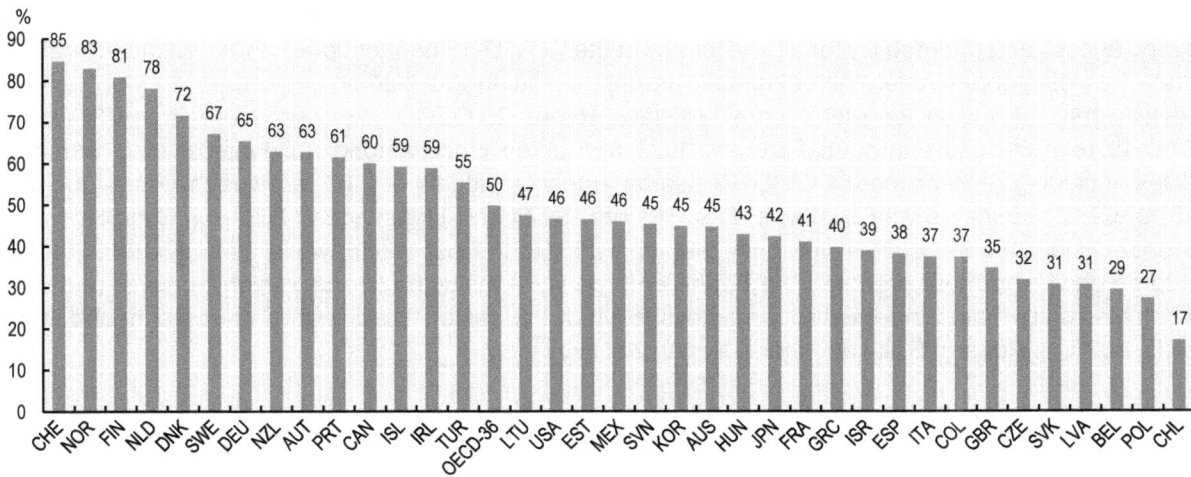

Source: OECD (2020[69]), *How's Life? 2020: Measuring Well-being*, https://dx.doi.org/10.1787/9870c393-en.

Over the course of the pandemic, people's trust in their government's response fell across most countries. The proportion of people reporting that they feel their government handled the coronavirus "well" or "somewhat well" declined on average across 11 OECD countries between March 2020 and March 2021, from 60% at the start of the pandemic to 46% by March 2021 (Figure 3.8). While the proportion of people who feel their government has responded well or somewhat well to the pandemic remains below spring 2020 levels in nearly all countries surveyed, confidence in the government response has increased steadily since spring 2021, possibly associated with rising vaccination rates and some relaxing of restrictions in spring-summer 2021 in many countries. By October 2021, 55% of people surveyed reported that they felt their governments were handling the pandemic well or somewhat well, a marked improvement from earlier in the year.

Figure 3.8. Proportion of people who feel their government is handling the coronavirus well or somewhat well

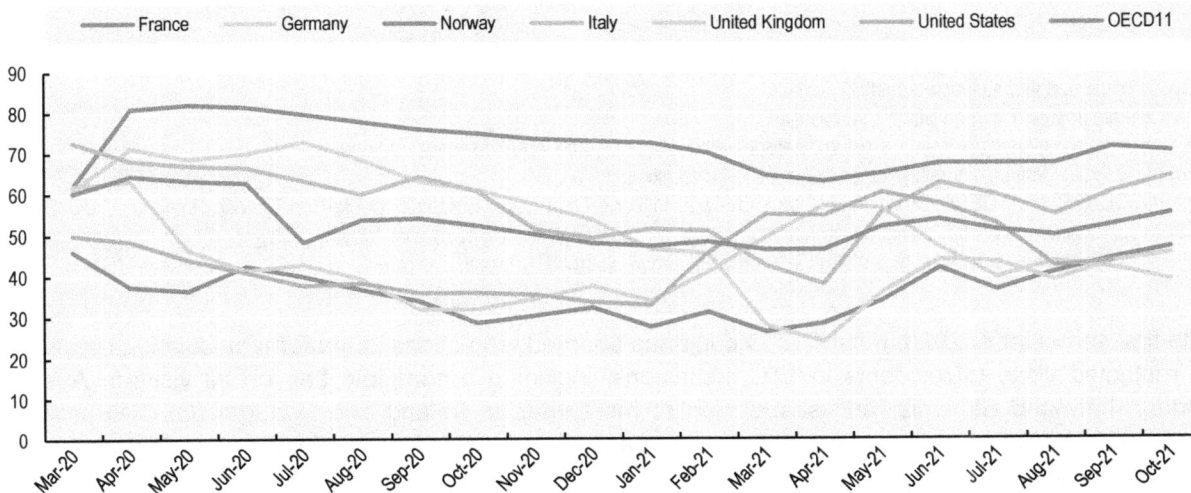

Note: In some cases, monthly averages were calculated by averaging multiple survey waves from the same month.
Source: YouGov (2021[70]), COVID-19 Public Monitor, https://yougov.co.uk/COVID-19.

The experience tackling the COVID-19 pandemic has severely tested health systems across OECD countries, and underscored how uneven progress towards people-centred care remains, despite important steps taken in recent years to put people at the centre. Reflecting the importance of better ensuring access and affordability for all, the impact of the COVID-19 pandemic – both in health and material terms – has disproportionately hit vulnerable groups, including low-income workers and older persons, especially those living in long-term care facilities. Across 25 OECD countries, more than 40% of all COVID-19 related deaths through February 2021 had taken place among residents of long-term care facilities, including 50% or more COVID-19 deaths among residents of LTC facilities in nearly one-third (8/25) of OECD countries with available data (Rocard, Sillitti and Llena-Nozal, 2021[71]). Long-term care was under-prioritised in health emergency planning prior to the pandemic, while staffing shortages and workforce challenges that predated the health emergency – including low pay, high turnover and skills mismatch – exacerbated pre-existing weaknesses when the sector faced such a dramatic health shock (OECD, 2020[72]; Rocard, Sillitti and Llena-Nozal, 2021[71]).

Figure 3.9. Proportion of all COVID-19 deaths occurring among long-term care residents

Share of COVID-19 deaths in LTC in all COVID-19 deaths (left scale); Number of COVID-19 deaths in LTC per million people aged 80 years and over (right scale)

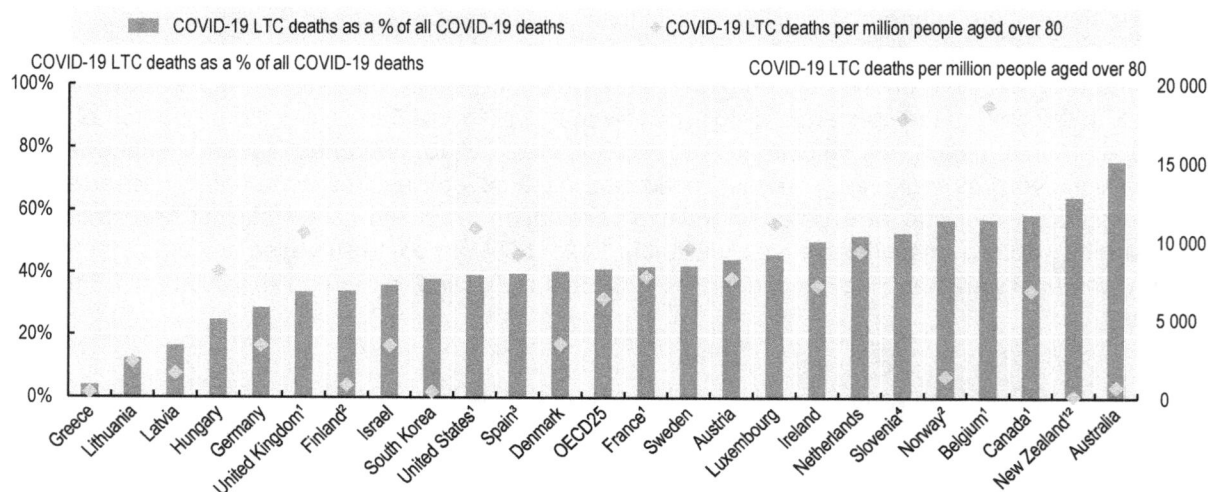

Note: Data on cumulative deaths up to early February 2021 (see Annex for details).
1. Includes confirmed and suspected deaths.
2. Only includes deaths occurring within LTC facilities.
3. Data come from regional governments using different methodologies, some including suspected deaths.
4. Slovenia includes deaths in nursing homes and social LTC facilities.
Source: OECD (2021[73]), OECD Questionnaire on COVID-19 in Long-Term Care; European Center for Disease Prevention and Control (2021[74]), Surveillance data from public online national reports on COVID-19 in long-term care facilities, https://www.ecdc.europa.eu/en/all-topics-z/coronavirus/threats-and-outbreaks/COVID-19/prevention-and-control/LTCF-data.

In the first semester of 2020, most OECD countries adopted restrictions in the form of isolation measures and restricted visits to residents in LTC institutions, including a complete ban on all visits in Austria, Hungary, Italy and Slovenia, and suspension of most visits in Ireland and Portugal (OECD/European Union, 2020[3]). While these restrictions have been associated with adverse effects on resident well-being in North America and Europe (Levere, Rowan and Wysocki, 2021[75]; Pitkälä, 2020[76]), there have also been reports of interventions introduced to mitigate these impacts. Innovations to increase resident social connections, improve physical fitness, promote communication between families and care staff or administrators, and support relationships between residents and staff have been reported in Canada, Japan, Spain, Switzerland, and the United States (Bowers et al., 2021[77]).

Building people-centred health systems: Lessons from COVID-19

As the magnitude of the impact of the COVID-19 pandemic became clearer in the first months of 2020, it may have seemed consensual among policy makers that some of the guiding principles of health systems would need to be placed on hold in the name of rapid containment of the spread of the virus. The cost of reducing patient involvement in decision-making, limiting choice and access to services, and dedicating the resources of health systems to treating COVID-19 patients, among other policies, may have seemed to be low in comparison to the potential death toll of the pandemic. However, after nearly two years of an enduring pandemic and its continuing effects, it is clear the principles of people-centredness remain a key approach to not only control the spread of infection but also to achieve the best possible health outcomes. Rather than being an obstacle, people-centredness should be seen as an asset of health systems in developing an effective response to COVID-19 and to other health shocks.

Some of the most important measures to contain the spread of the pandemic require high levels of participation and compliance from the part of the general public including, for example, the use of face masks, isolation of the infected, notification of contact cases, adherence to vaccination and proactive testing following the onset of symptoms. Similarly, successful outcomes in the continuity of care for all other conditions, especially non-communicable chronic diseases, also depend on principles of people-centredness, including ways to allow for people to be and remain active participants in their own treatments, developing and disseminating tools to allow for care to continue to be provided even during times of disruption, and promoting integrated delivery of care.

While health policy makers and health professionals did on some occasions correct course and develop more people-centred policies as the pandemic continued, the experience of the pandemic has shown that a people-centred approach should work far better when it is institutionalised far before a health shock hits. One definition of health systems resilience refers to their ability to absorb and minimise the effects of health shocks, while adapting and planning based on lessons learned for to ensure better performance in the future. With this perspective in mind, the COVID-19 pandemic offers many lessons to build more people-centred health systems going forward.

References

Al Jazeera (2021), *Canada launches COVID vaccine passport for travel*, https://www.aljazeera.com/news/2021/10/21/canada-launches-covid-vaccine-passport-for-travel. [35]

Badillo-Goicoechea, E. et al. (2021), *Global trends and predictors of face mask*. [23]

BBC (2021), *Covid vaccine to be mandatory for children in Costa Rica*, https://www.bbc.com/news/world-latin-america-59162510. [38]

Bencharif, S. (2021), *Belgium's new coronavirus measures: Schools targeted, bars left alone*, https://www.politico.eu/article/belgium-coronavirus-measures-covid19-alexander-de-croo-education/. [34]

Bhaskar, S. et al. (2020), "Telemedicine Across the Globe-Position Paper From the COVID-19 Pandemic Health System Resilience PROGRAM (REPROGRAM) International Consortium (Part 1)", *Frontiers in Public Health*, Vol. 8, http://dx.doi.org/10.3389/fpubh.2020.556720.   [11]

Bowers, B. et al. (2021), *What COVID-19 Innovations Can Teach Us About Improving Quality of Life in Long-Term Care*, Elsevier Inc., http://dx.doi.org/10.1016/j.jamda.2021.03.018.   [77]

Carrieri, V., L. Madio and F. Principe (2019), "Vaccine hesitancy and (fake) news: Quasi-experimental evidence from Italy", *Health Economics*, pp. 1377–1382, http://dx.doi.org/10.1002/hec.3937.   [28]

Chudasama, Y. et al. (2020), "Impact of COVID-19 on routine care for chronic diseases: A global survey of views from healthcare professionals", *Diabetes and Metabolic Syndrome: Clinical Research and Reviews*, Vol. 14/5, pp. 965-967, http://dx.doi.org/10.1016/j.dsx.2020.06.042.   [1]

de Goeij, H. (2021), *The Czech Republic prepares for new restrictions as cases soar*, https://www.nytimes.com/2021/11/18/world/europe/the-czech-republic-prepares-for-new-restrictions-as-cases-soar.html.   [39]

Dobiášová, K., Z. Kotherová and D. Numerato (2021), "Institutional reforms to strengthen patient and public involvement in the Czech Republic since 2014", *Health Policy*, http://dx.doi.org/10.1016/j.healthpol.2021.03.011.   [9]

El Pais (2021), *Certificado covid en España: qué comunidades han aprobado su uso y para qué actividades*, https://elpais.com/sociedad/2021-11-26/certificado-covid-que-comunidades-han-aprobado-su-uso-y-para-que-actividades.html.   [59]

El Pais (2021), *Covid passports: Which countries require them, and for what*, https://english.elpais.com/usa/2021-12-01/covid-passports-which-countries-require-them-and-for-what.html.   [43]

Euractiv (2021), *Fourth COVID-19 wave plateauing in Slovenia*, https://www.euractiv.com/section/politics/short_news/fourth-covid-19-wave-plateauing-in-slovenia/.   [58]

European Center for Disease Prevention and Control (2021), *Surveillance data from public online national reports on COVID-19 in long-term care facilities*, https://www.ecdc.europa.eu/en/all-topics-z/coronavirus/threats-and-outbreaks/COVID-19/prevention-and-control/LTCF-data.   [74]

European Patients Forum (2021), *Survey Report. The Impact of the COVID-19 Pandemic on Patients and Patient Organisations*, European Patients Forum, Brussels, http://www.eu-patient.eu.   [10]

Fan, J. et al. (2020), *The University of Maryland Social Data Science Center Global COVID-19 Trends and Impact Survey, in partnership with Facebook*, https://covidmap.umd.edu/api.html.   [22]

Federal Ministry of Social Affairs, Health Care and Consumer Protection (2021), *Questions and Answers: FAQ and contacts in relation to the EU Digital COVID Certificate in Austria*, https://gruenerpass.gv.at/en/faq/.   [32]

Fontanet, A. and S. Cauchemez (2020), *COVID-19 herd immunity: where are we?*, Nature Research, http://dx.doi.org/10.1038/s41577-020-00451-5.   [26]

France24 (2021), *Swiss voters back Covid pass law*, https://www.france24.com/en/live-news/20211128-swiss-voters-back-covid-pass-law. [61]

Gamble, A. et al. (2020), *The challenges of COVID-19 for people living with diabetes: Considerations for digital health*, JMIR Publications Inc., http://dx.doi.org/10.2196/19581. [65]

Garett, R. and S. Young (2021), "Online misinformation and vaccine hesitancy", *Translational Behavioral Medicine*, http://dx.doi.org/10.1093/tbm/ibab128. [29]

GEO (2021), *Covid-19 : le Portugal, rétablit plusieurs restrictions sanitaires*, https://www.geo.fr/voyage/covid-19-le-portugal-retablit-plusieurs-restrictions-sanitaires-207303. [56]

Government of Chile (2021), *Pase de Movilidad: Qué es el Pase de Movilidad?*, https://www.gob.cl/yomevacuno/pasemovilidad/. [36]

Government of the Netherlands (2021), *Where do I need to show a coronavirus entry pass?*, https://www.government.nl/topics/coronavirus-covid-19/covid-certificate/coronavirus-entry-pass/where-do-i-need-to-show-a-coronavirus-entry-pass. [53]

Government Offices of Sweden (2021), *The Government's work in response to the virus responsible for COVID-19*, https://www.government.se/government-policy/the-governments-work-in-response-to-the-virus-responsible-for-covid-1/. [60]

Haines, A. et al. (2020), "National UK programme of community health workers for", *The Lancet*, Vol. 395, pp. 1173-1175, http://dx.doi.org/10.1016/S0140-6736(20)30735-2. [67]

Hale, T. et al. (2021), "A global panel database of pandemic policies (Oxford COVID-19 Government Response Tracker)", *Nature Human Behaviour*, Vol. 5/4, pp. 529-538, http://dx.doi.org/10.1038/s41562-021-01079-8. [20]

Howard, J. et al. (2021), "An evidence review of face masks against COVID-19", *Proceedings of the National Academy of Sciences of the United States of America*, Vol. 118/4, http://dx.doi.org/10.1073/pnas.2014564118. [19]

Investment and Development Agency of Latvia (2021), *COVID-19 and traveling to Latvia*, https://www.latvia.travel/en/article/covid-19-and-travelling-latvia. [50]

Ipsos (2021), *Covid-19 Vaccination Intent. Ipsos survey for The World Economic Forum*. [27]

Ireland Department of the Taoiseach (2021), *Public health measures in place right now*, https://www.gov.ie/en/publication/3361b-public-health-updates/. [46]

Johnsen, T. et al. (2021), *Suitability of video consultations during the COVID-19 pandemic lockdown: Cross-sectional survey among Norwegian general practitioners*, JMIR Publications Inc., http://dx.doi.org/10.2196/26433. [16]

Kanta Services (2021), *COVID-19 Certificate and COVID-19 Passport*, https://www.kanta.fi/en/web/guest/covid-19-certificate. [42]

Köther, A., K. Siebenhaar and G. Alpers (2021), "Shared Decision Making during the COVID-19 Pandemic", *Medical Decision Making*, http://dx.doi.org/10.1177/0272989X211004147. [6]

Kriss.EE Government Communication Unit (2021), *Current restrictions*, https://www.kriis.ee/en/crisis-management-qa/crisis-management/current-restrictions. [41]

Kyodo News (2021), *Japan to lift spectator cap in easing of COVID-19 restrictions*, [48]
https://english.kyodonews.net/news/2021/11/fc70189e98bc-japan-to-lift-spectator-cap-in-easing-of-covid-19-restrictions.html.

Levere, M., P. Rowan and A. Wysocki (2021), "The Adverse Effects of the COVID-19 Pandemic [75]
on Nursing Home Resident Well-Being", *Journal of the American Medical Directors
Association*, Vol. 22/5, pp. 948-954.e2, http://dx.doi.org/10.1016/j.jamda.2021.03.010.

Liao, M. et al. (2021), "A technical review of face mask wearing in preventing respiratory COVID- [25]
19 transmission", *Current Opinion in Colloid & Interface Science*, Vol. 52, p. 101417,
http://dx.doi.org/10.1016/j.cocis.2021.101417.

Li, Y. and C. Sun (2021), "Face masks to prevent transmission of COVID-19: A systematic [24]
review and meta-analysis", *American Journal of Infection Control*, Vol. 49/7, pp. 900-906,
http://dx.doi.org/10.1016/j.ajic.2020.12.007.

Lockyer, B. et al. (2021), "Understanding COVID-19 misinformation and vaccine hesitancy in [30]
context: Findings from a qualitative study involving citizens in Bradford, UK", *Health
Expectations*, Vol. 24/4, pp. 1158-1167, http://dx.doi.org/10.1111/hex.13240.

Marin, A. (2020), "Telemedicine takes center stage in the era of COVID-19", *Science*, pp. 731- [12]
733, http://dx.doi.org/10.15585/mmwr.

Mehrotra, A. et al. (2021), *The Impact of COVID-19 on Outpatient Visits in 2020: Visits [14]
Remained Stable, Despite a Late Surge in Cases*, Commonwealth Fund, New York, NY,
http://dx.doi.org/10.26099/bvhf-e411.

Ministry of Health (2021), *COVID Certificate*, https://corona.health.gov.il/en/covid-certificate- [47]
lobby/covid-medical-certificate/.

Ministry of Health (2021), *My Covid Record: Proof of vaccination status*, [54]
https://www.health.govt.nz/our-work/diseases-and-conditions/covid-19-novel-
coronavirus/covid-19-vaccines/my-covid-record-proof-vaccination-status.

Ministry of the Economy and Innovation of the Republic of Lithuania (2021), *National Certificate*, [51]
https://eimin.lrv.lt/en/important-information-for-business-on-coronavirus-3/national-certificate.

Moore, A. and M. MacKenzie (2020), "Policy making during crises: How diversity and [8]
disagreement can help manage the politics of expert advice", *The BMJ*, Vol. 371,
http://dx.doi.org/10.1136/bmj.m4039.

Murphy, E. et al. (2020), "COVID-19: Public and patient involvement, now more than ever", *HRB [7]
Open Research*, Vol. 3, p. 35, http://dx.doi.org/10.12688/hrbopenres.13067.1.

Nationalt Kommunikations Partnerskab COVID-19 (2021), *Corona passport – where and how?*, [40]
https://en.coronasmitte.dk/corona-passport.

Nouvellet, P. et al. (2021), "Reduction in mobility and COVID-19 transmission", *Nature [18]
Communications*, Vol. 12/1, http://dx.doi.org/10.1038/s41467-021-21358-2.

Oderkirk, J. (2021), "Survey results: National health data infrastructure and governance", *OECD [68]
Health Working Papers*, No. 127, OECD Publishing, Paris,
https://dx.doi.org/10.1787/55d24b5d-en.

OECD (2021), "Enhancing public trust in COVID-19 vaccination: The role of governments", *OECD Policy Responses to Coronavirus (COVID-19)*, OECD Publishing, Paris, https://doi.org/10.1787/eae0ec5a-en. [31]

OECD (2021), *Health at a Glance 2021: OECD Indicators*, OECD Publishing, Paris, https://doi.org/10.1787/ae3016b9-en. [64]

OECD (2021), *OECD Questionnaire on COVID-19 in Long-Term Care*. [73]

OECD (2021), "Strengthening the frontline: How primary health care helps health systems adapt during the COVID 19 pandemic", *OECD Policy Responses to Coronavirus (COVID-19)*, OECD Publishing, Paris, https://doi.org/10.1787/9a5ae6da-en. [4]

OECD (2020), *How's Life? 2020: Measuring Well-being*, OECD Publishing, Paris, https://dx.doi.org/10.1787/9870c393-en. [69]

OECD (2020), *Who Cares? Atracting and Retaining Care Workers for the Elderly*, OECD Publishing, https://doi.org/10.1787/92c0ef68-en. [72]

OECD/European Union (2020), *Health at a Glance: Europe 2020: State of Health in the EU Cycle*, OECD Publishing, Paris, https://dx.doi.org/10.1787/82129230-en. [3]

Peretz, P., N. Islam and L. Matiz (2020), "Community Health Workers and Covid-19 — Addressing Social Determinants of Health in Times of Crisis and Beyond", *New England Journal of Medicine*, Vol. 383/19, p. e108, http://dx.doi.org/10.1056/nejmp2022641. [66]

Perrotta, D. et al. (2021), "Behaviours and attitudes in response to the COVID-19 pandemic: insights from a cross-national Facebook survey", *EPJ Data Science*, Vol. 10/1, http://dx.doi.org/10.1140/epjds/s13688-021-00270-1. [21]

Pitkälä, K. (2020), *COVID-19 has hit nursing homes hard*, Springer Science and Business Media Deutschland GmbH, http://dx.doi.org/10.1007/s41999-020-00411-1. [76]

Politico.EU (2021), *Greece toughens vaccine rules as coronavirus cases mount again*, https://www.politico.eu/article/greece-covid19-vaccination-booster-shots-europe-kyriakos-mitsotakis/. [44]

Reuters (2021), *Factbox: Countries making COVID-19 vaccines mandatory*, https://www.reuters.com/business/healthcare-pharmaceuticals/countries-making-covid-19-vaccines-mandatory-2021-08-16/. [45]

Reuters (2021), *Norway plans third vaccine dose for all adults, "corona passes"*, https://www.reuters.com/world/europe/norway-plans-third-covid-19-vaccine-dose-all-adults-2021-11-12/. [55]

Reuters (2021), *South Korea widens vaccine pass requirement as Omicron fears rise*, https://www.reuters.com/business/healthcare-pharmaceuticals/skorea-makes-vaccine-pass-mandatory-many-more-venues-omicron-fears-rise-2021-12-03/. [49]

Richardson, E. et al. (2020), "Keeping what Works: Remote Consultations during the COVID-19 Pandemic", *Eurohealth*, Vol. 26/2, https://apps.who.int/iris/handle/10665/336301. [15]

Richards, T. and H. Scowcroft (2020), "Patient and public involvement in covid-19 policy making", *The BMJ*, Vol. 370, http://dx.doi.org/10.1136/bmj.m2575. [5]

Rocard, E., P. Sillitti and A. Llena-Nozal (2021), "COVID-19 in long-term care: Impact, policy responses and challenges", *OECD Health Working Papers*, No. 131, OECD Publishing, Paris, https://dx.doi.org/10.1787/b966f837-en.　[71]

Schengeninfonews (2021), *Travel to Austria for Touristic Purposes Will Be Possible Again After December 13*, https://www.schengenvisainfo.com/news/travel-to-austria-for-touristic-purposes-will-be-possible-again-after-december-13/.　[33]

Terra Colombia (2021), *Mesures pour voyager en Colombie pendant le COVID-19*, https://www.voyage-colombie.com/pratique/infos-pratiques-covid-19.　[37]

The Lancet Oncology (2021), *COVID-19 and cancer: 1 year on*, Lancet Publishing Group, http://dx.doi.org/10.1016/S1470-2045(21)00148-0.　[2]

The Luxembourg Government (2021), *Coronavirus. Sanitary measures*, https://covid19.public.lu/en/sanitary-measures/restaurants-bars.html.　[52]

The Slovak Spectator (2021), *Green pass, Covid pass, Covid certificate. Which do you need when?*, https://spectator.sme.sk/c/22795067/green-pass-covid-pass-covid-certificate-which-do-you-need-when.html.　[57]

The Times (2021), *PM imposes plan B with working from home and Covid passports*, https://www.thetimes.co.uk/article/cabinet-rift-over-plan-for-vaccine-passports-r29vmv85l.　[63]

Turkish Ministry of the Interior (2021), *PCR test obligation for some activities*, https://www.icisleri.gov.tr/bazi-faaliyetler-icin-pcr-testi-zorunlulugu-genelgesi-gonderildi.　[62]

Weiner, J. et al. (2021), "In-Person and Telehealth Ambulatory Contacts and Costs in a Large US Insured Cohort Before and During the COVID-19 Pandemic", *JAMA network open*, Vol. 4/3, p. e212618, http://dx.doi.org/10.1001/jamanetworkopen.2021.2618.　[13]

Whaley, C. et al. (2020), "Changes in Health Services Use among Commercially Insured US Populations during the COVID-19 Pandemic", *JAMA Network Open*, Vol. 3/11, http://dx.doi.org/10.1001/jamanetworkopen.2020.24984.　[17]

YouGov (2021), *COVID-19 Public Monitor*, https://yougov.co.uk/covid-19.　[70]

www.ingramcontent.com/pod-product-compliance
Lightning Source LLC
Chambersburg PA
CBHW080620270326
41928CB00016B/3140